DESTINATION DACHSHUND

Three Months, Three Generations
& Sixty Dachshunds

DESTINATION DACHSHUND

A Travel Memoir

Three Months, Three Generations & Sixty Dachshunds

LISA FLEETWOOD

First published in 2016

Copyright © 2016 Lisa Fleetwood

www.lisafleetwood.com.au

Disclaimer: Many of the historical details mentioned in this novel are what the author recorded at the time from information provided by tour guides and may not be an accurate representation of history.

Bookends Publishing
Sydney, Australia
www.bookendspublishing.com.au

Edited by Nancy Pile
Cover illustration & sign post by Sillier Than Sally Designs

National Library of Australia
Cataloguing-in-Publication data:
Fleetwood, Lisa
Destination dachshund : a travel memoir : three months, three generations & sixty dachshunds / Lisa Fleetwood.
http://trove.nla.gov.au/version/229013676

ISBN-13: 978-0-9945914-0-1 (pbk.)

This book is dedicated to a few—
My dad, who should have been with us on this journey of a
lifetime with three generations.

Anthony, my hardworking and incredibly generous husband,
without whom this trip would never have been possible in our
wildest dreams.

And finally, my darling Coco, and all the dachshunds we have
loved.

*One's destination is never a place
but rather a new way of looking at things.*

—Henry Miller

INTRODUCTION

'You're travelling for three months with your parents? Really?'

This may come as a surprise to my mother and parents-in-law when they read this, but when my husband, Anthony, and I told people we were travelling abroad for three months with our parents, they thought we were crazy.

'People do this,' I kept telling everyone, 'They do—people take long trips with their families—it isn't uncommon.'

Anthony and I were confident it would work. We all got along well; there was no firecracker amongst us, no loud talker, no know-it-all. We had well-behaved parents is what I'm saying, and we *knew* it would work. *They're family.* We could spend three months with them, surely.

Three Months

A short trip has its advantages, but if you can swing it, whether it's caravanning, hiring an RV to drive across the country, or overseas travel, a long trip offers valuable extended time with your family, even if it's only once in your life.

To the astonishment of a lot of people, we were also leaving the lovely Australian spring and summer to journey to the Northern

1

Hemisphere and venture into the cold. Were we skiing? No. Were we visiting family? No. So why go then? Why not wait and experience the Northern summer?

It was simple. The holiday coincided with the children's end of year school holidays (long summer break over Christmas). But there were added advantages: there are fewer tourists at that time of year, and there is just something *so* magical about Europe in the lead up to Christmas. I'm a sucker for Christmas markets. And if it happened to snow lightly, while I ambled with a mulled wine, past gable-roofed stalls selling Christmas ornaments, then, joy to the world!

Three Generations

The holiday had been two years in the planning and started out with just the four of us—Anthony and me and our two children, Samuel and Holly. But because my father passed away unexpectedly of pneumonia after being diagnosed with lung cancer, we asked my mum, Patricia, along and soon after, Anthony's parents, Maree and David. And although this multi-generational journey would not have come about if Dad hadn't died, the fact he wasn't here to enjoy it with us was heartbreaking.

In travelling with three generations, the children would have extra time with their grandparents, *valuable time*, time I wished they could have had with my dad. And Anthony and I would have more time to spend with our parents and children; *relaxed* time spent exploring and seeing the world.

Two Dachshunds

But there are downsides to three months of travel—leaving our pets. And for us, it was our two-year-old miniature dachshunds, Coco and Charlie. The thought of leaving them caused many tears in the weeks leading up to the departure. We knew they'd be well cared for by good friends who were house and dog-sitting, but it didn't make leaving them any easier, as we're a little obsessed with dachshunds and always have been.

Dachshunds are big in my family, you see. My grandparents owned one, my family had them, and then so did I.

I met Anthony when I was twenty, this man who would soon become my husband. I viewed him as a perfect match for three reasons. He had the full trifecta. He was cute, he was funny, and he loved dachshunds. And not only did he love dachshunds, *his* family had owned them for years too. Seriously, it was kismet.

After marrying my dachshund-loving man, of course we got our own fur baby—a cheeky, brown miniature dachshund, and two years later, we got another. But time passed and our puppies aged, like they are supposed to, like we are *all* supposed to. They lived long, full lives but to our great sadness they died in 2010.

It was too quiet, though, I'd had dogs my whole life, and this was my first time without any since I was a very young child. Dogs fill my day with endless joy and share unconditional love that never wavers, so within a month I was searching for puppies. Eight weeks later, we had two new miniature dachshunds, Coco and Charlie. We loved them, and they loved us—and if we thought we'd been mad about dachshunds before, looking back, I realise this was when our true obsession started.

Our three-month journey was to be one of excitement and adventure, exploring the world and spending quality time with our children and parents, but little did I know that the trip would be about *so* much more than family, our human family anyway.

1

SYDNEY, AUSTRALIA

Almost Go-Time

With only a week to go, the excitement is building in the House of Fleetwood. As Anthony has always had a busy job and worked long hours, he is looking forward to three months off. And I am eager to be away—I'm tired of organising the holiday and just want to be on it.

Our parents, Patricia (my mum) and Maree and David (Anthony's parents) are so thrilled to be going on such a big trip that they've been packed for weeks. The kids, Sam and Holly, whose end-of-year exams are right around the time of our departure, are excited as we're leaving halfway through them. What child wouldn't be?

The last year has been filled with planning, spreadsheets, and charting itineraries. There are so many details to check with a tailored itinerary for three months of travel I develop a computer-induced hunchback-like appearance. I can safely say there wasn't any creative writing done in the year prior to the trip. It's a shame the holiday-planning-razor-sharp-focus doesn't transfer to other aspects of my life. Most of the time I am off with the fairies in a place where selective deafness and forgetfulness is the real me. My husband loves it—just ask him.

Coco and Charlie follow me everywhere. Especially Coco, as she knows something is up. She has this uncanny way of knowing when a bag has been packed, so she becomes my little shadow in the days before we are due to leave. The dogs get away with sitting on the lounge and cuddling in bed with us, and I know it's going to be so hard to leave them. Holly constantly asks whether we can take them with us, and at twelve, I know she knows it isn't possible, but it doesn't stop her from asking.

We pop out for a few hours to visit friends, and while we are gone, death slithers into our yard and takes something precious from us.

For the Love of Dachshunds

We return from our outing to find only Charlie at the gate to greet us. At first I'm not worried—we live on an acre. Coco must be around the back somewhere. Ten minutes later, we're still looking.

Anthony calls my name. I turn and the look on his face tells me something is wrong. He and Holly are standing near a garden, and I can see that whatever Anthony knows, Holly does not. It's not until I walk over and see Coco laying under a shrub that I let out a wail. I stomp at the ground. I shake my head. All I can say is *no*. It's the only word my mind can grasp.

No, no, no, no, no.

It's then Holly understands that Coco is not merely sleeping in the shade. It is heartbreaking to watch the realisation wash over her face.

I can't breathe. I feel as though a boulder sits heavy on my chest.

Sam joins us, and with disbelief the four of us crouch around our precious girl. Charlie sniffs at Coco and jumps at us. He is skittish, like a horse. He knows something is wrong.

Coco lies quietly before us out of the heat of the sun. She hasn't been there long. Anthony and I suspect a snakebite, and I can't help thinking if we'd been home even half an hour earlier, we may have had time to take her to the vet to have the antivenom administered.

We've had snakes on the property before, but not this early—it's usually the hotter months that snakes are a problem, from December to March, and we aren't prepared for snakes, not yet. We aren't prepared for death, not now.

Minutes later, while the kids are in my arms, Anthony finds a dead adult red-belly black snake not far away. Coco, our little dog weighing no more than five kilos, had taken on this big snake but lost her life in the process. I pick her up and cradle her to my chest. I can't yet comprehend that she is gone.

And as for Charlie, he is cuddled continuously, collecting up the rolling tears on our cheeks with his tongue. He won't leave our side or our laps. When it comes to nighttime on the first day, he won't stay in his bed. Within minutes his howls break our hearts, and Holly spends the night with him.

The next night he is the same. And during the day, he lies in his bed with his head on his paws, staring at us with his glossy brown eyes. We give him a stuffed brown dog that normally would have had its stuffing removed within minutes, but not this time. He just cuddles up to the dog like he would Coco. He looks for Coco everywhere, sniffing near where we found her, in their bed, and around the house. He can't be alone without barking and is so miserable I take him to the vet, who prescribes doggy anxiety tablets.

It is only days until our departure. I am stressed and busy with packing, organising household bills, last-minute confirmation emails to the hotels and tours booked in the first weeks of the holiday. Anthony is busy finalising as much as he can at work. The kids have exams. There are tears, a lot of tears, and there is silence. And there is Charlie, our gorgeous boy who was the quieter of the two dogs. Coco was the beggar of food, the scratcher at the door, the one we would find up on the lounge sunning herself where she wasn't supposed to be. Charlie is the quiet one, and quieter now without her.

I numbly arrange Coco's cremation, collect her ashes in a beautiful timber box, and organise for a jacaranda tree to be planted to remember her by.

I cry and then cry some more, as does the rest of the family. This is not right, this trip we'd been planning for two years wasn't supposed to be starting with tears and clutching a black dachshund in our arms like he was going to disappear in a puff of smoke.

Holly does not want to leave Charlie, and I spend hours talking her around. I know he'll be well cared for while we are away. I tell myself over and over again how lucky we are to be going on a holiday of this epic scale. We have to go.

Dog lovers will understand, others may think, 'It's just a dog,' but for us, our dachshunds are part of our family. We love them. And we loved Coco, the cheeky tan dachshund who stole our hearts with her beautiful brown eyes and crazy antics.

Death can come at any time, and indeed it did with Coco and my dad. Life needs to be embraced, so we go through the motions, and we pack and prepare to leave.

Our first stop is Singapore.

(2)

SINGAPORE

Date: October 19
Location: Sydney – Singapore
Nights: 1
Dachshunds so far: 0

Leaving Charlie

Seven huge suitcases are loaded into the van, seven backpacks and seven excited people. But I feel unsettled and not at all how I thought I'd be feeling. Charlie isn't quite himself yet, and it doesn't feel right to leave him only days after Coco's death. Instead of smiles as we drive out of our front gates, for Holly and me especially, there are tears. But we wave goodbye to Charlie, who is in the arms of Angela, our friend and neighbour, and we watch, necks craned, until he disappears from view.

Leaving Charlie is hard, but now that we're on our way, excitement takes ahold of me. And how could I not be happy? Anthony and I are about to embark on a once-in-a-lifetime trip. By 'once-in-a-lifetime,' I mean a trip with our children and parents. We have three seventy year-olds and two teenage children with us—this is never going to happen again—not like this.

Our parents will continue to age and won't cope with a trip of this scale in the future. The children will not stop growing, and before long they'll have their own lives. I know this is the only time we'll travel like this—with the three generations—so I need to make the most of it. I turn and grin madly at Holly hoping to lure her into some smile therapy, and after a minute of crazy smiling, we're both laughing.

'I miss Coco and Charlie,' Holly whispers.

'I know, me too,' I respond, 'but the trip will go so fast, and we'll be back here with Charlie before you know it.'

'Can we Skype Charlie?'

'It's already organised.'

I sit back and relax into my seat. After two years from our first discussion about the trip, we're finally on our way.

Eighty-Eight Days

Anthony, a seasoned business traveller, is laid back in the Qantas Lounge. He is used to this and acts super cool in his Blues Brothers t-shirt, sipping his tea and reading the paper, while the rest of us pose for photos and collect plates full of snacks and pots of tea and pancakes.

Holly attempts to teach me an elaborate clapping game called 'Concentration' that involves thinking of girls' or boys' names starting with different letters of the alphabet while we clap. I fail miserably. She then tries to teach the grandparents the game, and they are even worse.

'Is it too early for champagne?' I think. 'Probably.' But I have one anyway, as not only is this the first day of our adventure, but it's also Mum's birthday. We clink glasses together and smile.

Her birthday this year covers two times zones and is twenty-eight hours long, so she celebrates by having four wines on the flight. Sam and Anthony enter the in-flight movie zone and are not seen until the end of the flight. Maree and David are smiling in their seats like two kids winning a truckload of lollies, and in between giggling with Holly and watching a movie I put away two more champagnes, a wine, and a Baileys. But who's counting? I'm on holiday! For eighty-eight days!

We arrive at our hotel in steamy Singapore, and after check-in, we all do the single most important thing after dumping bags and visiting the loo. A refreshing beverage? No, that can wait. Wi-Fi is what we're searching for. From grandparents to kids, it is one of the first things we attend to. What have we turned into?

What is the code?
Is it free?
My iPad won't connect!
Which network are you using?
Why can't I get in?

Will it be the last time we hear these questions? No, not by a long shot.

As soon as I'm online, there's a message from Angela, who is minding Charlie for the first two weeks of our trip. She informs us that Charlie has left a present in her bedroom—a poo. He is such a kind and generous dog to give such a gift.

He does that sometimes, our Charlie, when he can't find us in the house. I see it as 'abandonment retaliation.' A kind of—Where were you when I wanted you? It's like he is trying to say, 'I searched and searched the whole house and NOTHING. You were nowhere. Therefore, I shall poo in your bedroom.'

Angela's message makes us laugh, of course, but Holly and I need to hug it out as we're missing Charlie already. My thoughts turn to Coco and how hard it's going to be to return home and not hear her yippy sounds of excitement or have her crawl up around the back of my neck and curl around me like a fox fur stole. Tears sting in my eyes. I can't stop picturing her in the garden, can't stop thinking about her dying on her own.

Mum, Maree, and I connect with home via email and phone, and my sister Karen wishes Mum a happy birthday. Facebook is checked. Pictures are sent. What did we do before the Internet? No, seriously I want to know. Tell me. Now.

Isn't This Nice?

Our first foray into Singapore is in search for food. I am embarrassed to say the first stop for nourishment on our big trip is KFC. Hungry teenage boys need to be fed and fast, but the rest of us eat elsewhere.

It is then, on a busy sidewalk, that I take my first official overseas photo. It is of two little white dogs in a basket on the front of a man's bike, each wearing a little puppy helmet on their heads. This causes instant excitement from the kids. The man on the bicycle checks his dogs, making sure they are secure, and I snap a few photos before he rides off.

We decide to visit Clarke Quay for dinner, which is a short walk from the hotel in the early evening. Although the oppressive heat of the day has eased, it's still humid. The full moon is shining brightly over the city skyline. As we walk along the Singapore River, small red, green, and yellow boats whizz by, their brightly lit lanterns leaving shining streaks in my photographs.

I later find out these boats are called 'Bumboats.' It's a shame we don't have more time in Singapore, as I would very much like to say I've been on a Bumboat, although I'm disappointed there are no bums in sight.

Mum and I stop to take photos of the pretty lights and buildings along the quay. Our photos are lovely, but this thirty-second photo op means we lose sight of Anthony, who is walking ahead. The quay is busy, and the farther we walk, the more people there are milling around. There are rides and acrobats and crowds that suck up family members like a vacuum from Hell.

Great. Our first walk as a group, and we're separated. I realise we need an actual plan for walking in crowds, especially when the only person with a phone is me and the only person with a map is Anthony. Eventually we find each other, and Anthony and I have a discussion about the people walking behind keeping up vs. the people in front waiting when someone is taking a photo. I have a funny feeling this will not be the last time this talk takes place.

Sitting under shining red and gold lanterns, we enjoy noodle soup, a prawn omelet, beef noodles, and 'Happy birthday!' cheers, preceded by my most common phrase while on holidays, 'Isn't this nice?'

I say this so often nobody in my immediate family—Anthony, Sam, and Holly—answers anymore. Don't they realise I am going to force them to answer? Get used to it people—we have eighty-eight days of this.

I crawl into bed with Anthony on our first day, tired but happy, and start the first entry of my travel blog. But before long Holly creeps into our room and into our bed for a cuddle. She is missing Charlie and Coco. So am I.

To Infinity's Edge

The next morning sees us dip into the humidity of Singapore again for a walk around Merlion Park. The park curls around the wide bay, lined with trees and pathways.

'Any dachshunds?' I ask Anthony, who is gazing intently around the park.

'Not yet,' he replies, 'Too hot.'

I agree. I know dachshunds; they're fairly lazy, so I don't think our usual holiday dachshund spotting competition is going to kick off here in this heat. But you never know. Jangle a lead, slide a knife across a chopping board, or crinkle a packet of *any* type of food, and any seemingly lazy dachshund will go from a deep sleep to a high level of excitement in a nanosecond.

The first stop on our walk is at the spectacular Merlion, a seventy-tonne half-fish, half-lion water fountain rising 8.6 metres into the air from a blue- and white-tiled wave. It majestically spouts water in an arching stream into the somewhat murky water of the bay. Tourists crowd the area, posing for photos with outstretched hands as though capturing the water.

I'm smitten with the Merlion, Singapore's national icon. I want one. Who wouldn't? I wonder if anyone would notice if I tried to smuggle it on the plane . . . although it may tip the scales on our bag limit.

Maree, David, and Mum press on through the heat, but a stop for water and a rest is needed halfway to our destination of the Marina Bay Sands Hotel. It gleams brightly in the sun on the other side of the bay, three curved towers supporting a ship up in the air, like three twisting waves.

With sighs of relief, we finally enter the air-conditioning of the Marina Bay Sands complex and make our way to the reception of the Sands SkyPark Observation Deck. It is a cool 152 Australian dollars to check out the view over Singapore.

After an hour walking in the exhausting heat to find it costs a night's accommodation, it prompts a discussion about the merits of this view and will it be worth it. It's one of those holiday things people talk themselves into, though. After a forced group tourist photo with a fake Singapore backdrop that we won't buy, we enter the lift.

The views over Singapore on this blue-sky day are, in fact, beautiful. The skyline and the waters of the bay and ocean sparkle in the sun. Farther out, there are so many boats and ships in the South China Sea I can't count them all. From the Merlion to the high-rise buildings and soaring treetops of the Gardens by the Bay, it is worth the price of the ticket. It's brilliant, as is the blue pool sweeping around to our left. What would make the view even more brilliant is if we could all throw ourselves in the Marina Bay Sands infinity pool, fully clothed.

Holly's gaze is not on the views but the pool. She asks several times if she can go in, but as far as I know, only hotel guests can relax in the expensive waters. She asks why we couldn't have stayed here, and Anthony responds, 'We're not made of money.'

'But,' Holly insists, 'it has an infinity edge pool!'

She's obviously forgotten *we* have an infinity edge pool at home. Apparently the 1.2-metre drop to our backyard is not quite as impressive as the Titanic-like Marina Bay Sands pool. What?

Our last stop in Singapore before it's time to leave for the airport is the National Orchid Garden, which is serious catnip for old ladies. (Nothing wrong with old ladies—one day I'll be one, and I will own it!) It's lush, tranquil, and vibrant and offers shady bowers that are a refreshing reprieve from the heat.

Holly makes her first holiday purchase, a tiny orchid ornament. We buy what will be the first of many Christmas ornaments purchased on the trip. I plan for our Christmas tree in New York City, where we'll be come 25th December, to be a bright display of our travels.

Singapore is one of only a few places on the trip where we need summer clothes, but honestly we could have done with no clothes at all. It is sweltering hot and one of the main reasons I prefer travelling in the cooler months. It would be different if we were relaxing by a pool, but when on a touring holiday, I would much rather get about rugged up in the whole jeans-beanie-scarf-gloves-duck-down-jacket-thick-socks-boots combo than be a tourist in the heat.

Singapore—you rock, especially your impressive Merlion, but when I return to your beautiful shores, it will be to swim in the Marina Bay Sands Hotel infinity pool, drink cocktails, and view your city from above.

And so we reach the end of Day 1 and begin our first experience of packing up, checking for chargers, and checking out. And except for getting separated at Clarke Quay, so far so good.

Not a dachshund in sight. Probably too hot for them.

(3)

ISTANBUL, TURKEY

Date: *October 21*
Location: *Singapore – Istanbul*
Nights: *4*
Dachshunds so far: *0*

Welcome to Cat City

Ahmet, our guide for the next ten days, picks us up at Ataturk Airport. He is a friendly man and very helpful. Although I've travelled a fair bit, I've never been on an organised tour. I'm not used to someone being there to tell us where to go, check us into hotels, and make sure we're comfortable. I have to say—I don't mind it! I'll take advantage of it because after Turkey we are on our own.

Our first night in Singapore was in adjoining rooms with Mum. However, as we unpack in Istanbul, I'm conscious of Mum being on her own, so between Holly, Maree, and me, we make sure she has some company here and there. She copes well on her own and is used to her own company, but it doesn't change the fact that her partner of so many years is gone and all the things they used to do together, no matter how small, like unpacking or delighting over a nice hotel room, she now does on her own.

We hit the streets, eager to look around. It is busy with cars and trams whizzing by. Ahead, far ahead, I can see water, but more immediately the sidewalks are crammed with men in groups selling all sorts of things from fake handbags to perfume to arts and crafts. Saying, 'No thank you,' politely we move on, but some follow, calling out prices or offering other objects to sell.

We pass shops selling tinted-glass lights and Turkish delight. There are food carts selling kebabs and pides, and cafes filled with people smoking from tall water pipes.

We buy Turkish delight at a cafe, an expensive treat of cubed, dark red jelly covered in a dusting of powdered sugar. It is liked by some and not by others.

The closer we come to the Old City, the crowds thin out, and the cats take their place. I've never seen so many stray cats in one spot. They don't bother anyone, they're just lazing about in the pretty Sultanahmet Park in the afternoon sun, along with a fair few dogs. We look for dachshunds, even though they're probably not the stray kind, but none are spotted. We also see a man casually walking a brown and white goat and one Merlion. Just kidding, it's in Singapore.

The towering domes and minarets of the historic Sultan Ahmet Mosque pierce the skyline, and I can't wait to explore Istanbul over the next two days, but everyone knows what the best part about Turkey is going to be for Holly—cats. And the answer to Holly's burning question of 'Can I pat them?' is a resounding, 'NO.'

Strong Bonds

Anthony finds a place for dinner, not far from our hotel. At first glance it looks like a takeaway place, and as my friends know, I don't mind a glass of wine with dinner. But tonight it is Coke or Coke.

Although the food is tasty and the waiters are friendly, the atmosphere around the restaurant is not so great. It is noisy with cars from the main road, and street sellers lean over our table, attempting to sell perfume, leather jackets, spinning tops, socks, shirts, and packets of tissues. We are all too nice though, responding, 'No thank you,' politely and continuing with our meal and conversation. I silently wish Dad were here as he would have told them to piss off.

Mum and I share a glance as the food arrives. Dad would have enjoyed this meal. He loved his food, loved talking to people, and would entice amazing meals from restaurateurs that were family recipes and not on the menu. We're served large platters of grilled meats, salads, kebabs, flatbread, and eggplant, along with plates of hot chips, followed by apple-flavoured Turkish tea in hourglass glass teacups with little clumps of sugar and tiny silver spoons. The kids sip the tea gingerly with screwed up faces as though it's poison. It's not their 'cup of tea' apparently.

Mum and I slip into nice, comfy chairs in the hotel bar for a wine and chat after dinner as the others file up to bed. Maree isn't much of a drinker, but joins us for a little while before heading upstairs after promising to join us for a wine next time.

Tonight, as a family, Anthony, Sam, Holly, and I settle into our first hotel room together for the trip. Anthony snuggles in bed with Holly, earphones shared between them, laughing away together at

21

the inappropriate jokes on the TV show *Cougar Town*. Sam sits close by reading. I watch them all for a few minutes, feeling like the luckiest woman in the world.

At home, we are often spread all over the house in separate rooms, especially now the kids are growing older. But on a holiday, one of my favourite things is being all in together. There is no escape from each other. There are more cuddles, more jokes, and the children only have each other to play with. They may not realise it now, it may come to them later in life, but their shared experiences and time spent one-on-one as children on these extended holidays will, I hope, create a strong bond. Fingers crossed.

Spices, Cats, and Rubber Ducks

Established between 1597 and 1664, the Spice Bazaar, or Egyptian Bazaar, is in a stunning building near the Bosphorus waterfront. It is clean and tidy with lovely little shopfronts and polite, friendly people. I thought the bazaar would be noisy and dirty, and we'd be hassled, but we're not.

I'm pleasantly surprised, and I don't mean with the Turkish people, not at all; everyone we've come across so far has been nice, except maybe some of the more forceful street sellers. They seem to target the ladies and especially Holly, with her blonde hair, and I do find them a little intimidating. I've been to markets in Bali and Vietnam, and in various markets in both countries, there isn't much respect for personal space. My arms were grabbed guiding me into shops to which I would resist. I tell you right now, marketeers of the world—I am more likely to buy your wares if you refrain from touching me.

As we meander down the wide pathways below arched ceilings, the aroma is of spices and coffee and more spices. Rich colours burst from everywhere—from the vibrant orange and yellow of paprika, turmeric, and cumin to fabrics, lamps, water pipes, and jewellery in an array of colours. There are shining silver tea sets, apple tea and Turkish delight, hanging lengths of dried peppers, garlic, and corn, clothes, rugs, and souvenirs. We buy bookmarks, key rings, and sparkly bracelets while Sam barters for a fez hat that he will probably never wear again.

The weather is stunning outside with bright blue sky above. The shining sun warms us as we embark on a cruise along the Bosphorus Strait, the wide stretch of water separating the continents of Europe and Asia. The views back over Istanbul and the main dome, six minarets, and eight smaller domes of the Sultan Ahmet Mosque dominate the skyline. As the boat starts, Ahmet waves us up to the huge upper deck and takes to the microphone. We all look around, wondering where all the other people are, and then we realise it's just the seven of us on a boat large enough for about 250.

When I booked our private tour of Turkey, I knew it would be the seven of us with our guide and minivan, but I wasn't expecting a private boat. Ha! The grandparents are impressed. We settle in and look to the shore for what will be one of the most memorable moments of the trip for me. Relaxed and happy, we snap photos of each other and the scenery.

It's lovely to see Anthony having fun with the kids and his parents. He is beginning to relax, but he's not quite there yet, as there are still work things occupying his mind. But for now, he is in the sun with his arms around the kids and a smile on his face. I sit with them and look at the water. No matter where we travel, I always find our outings on the water the moments I look back on the most.

David, my father-in-law, who is in Rotary International, has brought the Rotary rubber ducky on the trip. He holds it up for its first photo of the holiday with the waters of the Bosphorus behind its plastic yellow form.

The boat cuts through the choppy, blue waters of the Bosphorus Strait with the bright red Turkish flag fluttering on the stern. We spy mansions, schools, palaces, fortresses, mosques, and an open-air nightclub. I try to con Anthony into going to the nightclub with me later, but I'd be more likely to get him to go skydiving, and he hates heights.

After the tour we scoff down tasty kebabs wrapped in foil from a street vendor before wandering along sloping cobblestone, tree-lined streets. We pass busy cafes, rug shops, and cats, all the way to the impressive gates of the Istanbul Archeology Museum. At Holly's insistence—museums are her all-time favourite—not really, but being such awful parents we subject her to a couple of hours of 'boring old stuff' where she quickly announces she is 'feeling sick and really tired' (code for 'really bored').

We all laugh at this. It's a running joke after our trip to Europe in 2009 where Holly, then eight, announced she was 'really sick and tired' while looking through the world-renowned Uffizi Gallery in Florence. Funnily enough, she recovered almost instantly after exiting the art gallery . . .

Having already been to Italy and Greece, we've done our share of archeological museums, and for the adults, roaming around and gazing at ancient tombs, Roman statues, and artifacts from early civilizations is a nice way to spend the afternoon, but for the kids, after a cursory glance over the museum's offerings, looking for cats outside in the surrounding gardens and performing legendary jumps from the steps of the museum is *way* more interesting.

We descend on the Kent Hotel buffet for dinner, where my mother-in-law Maree joins Mum and me for that promised wine. She has two, which is one more than her usual amount, and is quite giggly. She declares she is a 'one-wine kind of woman.' Mum and I decide that over the course of three months, we can morph Maree into a 'two-wines kind of woman.'

Maree bargains with Mum, 'If you have a cup of tea and cake with me in the morning, then I'll have a wine with you in the afternoon.'

Mum smiles, affirming, 'It's a deal.'

It's so lovely to see an extra level of friendship forming between Mum and Maree, and David too. They've always been friendly, of course, being the parents of two such fabulous children as Anthony and I (ha!). And they were probably always going to get on, but this is the first time in the twenty years Anthony and I've been married that they've spent any more time together than a dinner, lunch, or party, so it's nice to see their growing friendship.

History Lessons with Ahmet

According to our knowledgeable guide Ahmet, October is the best time to visit Turkey, so bonus for us. We have the nice weather but without the thousands of tourists. Usually there are six or seven cruise ships in port, which means busloads of people lining up at the tourist attractions. Can I point out why travelling in off-peak is better?

Firstly we are driven to the Sultan Ahmet Mosque, known to Westerners as the Blue Mosque because of the blue-tiled ceiling. We all remove shoes, and the ladies must don headscarves that may have been used by hundreds of tourists before us. I have no problem with the scarf wearing—happy to go with the local religious custom—but had I been pre-warned, I would have brought my own scarf.

Built from 1609 to 1616 with over 20 thousand handmade Iznik ceramic tiles arranged in beautiful designs of flowers and fruit, and two hundred stained glass windows, the interior of the Blue Mosque is truly awesome to see. It is busy at the mosque as tourist visits are timed to fall between the five prayer sessions of the day, and it closes for ninety minutes for each session.

Next up is the gloriously medieval-looking Hagia Sofia, built on the site of a pagan temple to Artemis. It was once a Christian church, then a mosque, and now a museum. The interior is a mix of Muslim and Christian influences. Islamic images sit side-by-side with depictions of Christ. Inside there are nooks and crannies, uneven steps, and shadowed hallways, all of which give it a dark, medieval feel. It's rough around the edges and needs repair but is still beautiful and eerie. Great place to film a thriller!

We have some family time afterwards in the courtyard cafe outside the Hagia Sophia, with tea and cake, and rounds of clapping with Holly playing Concentration. I am becoming better at calling out boys' and girls' names at the same time as tricky sequences of clapping. Not great, but better.

We then line up in the long lines to the toilets (for the women anyway). There are never queues for the men's toilet. In my opinion, toilet stops are the bane of any traveller, anywhere. And with four ladies who go twice as much as the men, the need for toilet stops is a regular and not very interesting discussion. But we have one rule: if there is a toilet, you go, because inevitably when the need arises, there will not be a toilet within cooee.

Ahmet leads us beneath the city and into the subterranean Basilica Cistern, a sixth century water supply that was once filled by ancient aqueducts (pipes) that carried water from nineteen kilometres away. It is dark, with uplighting at the base of the 336 columns. These columns march in precision, twelve rows of twenty-eight columns, in what is quite a large space. There is the constant *drip, drip, drip* of water, damp stone, and cool air.

As we follow the timber platform, it sparks my writerly imagination. I feel like I'm inside a Dan Brown novel, and everywhere I look I expect to see a murderous albino or a tweed-wearing professor on the run, checking his Mickey Mouse watch as he races past, over-explaining everything he sees.

To my great disappointment there is no albino and no Tom Hanks—and I may have my Dan Brown novels mixed up—but still, there is something fantastical about the cistern and its moss-covered columns.

We then visit the Topkapi Palace, down near the waterfront as well as all the neighbourhood cats. *Cats! Cats! Cats! See your cats HERE!* Again, I will point out that they are quite nice cats. And no, Holly, you are still not allowed to pat them . . .

Topkapi Palace is the palace and grounds of the former sultans, sitting on seven hundred acres overlooking the stunning blue waters of the Bosphorus Strait. We pose together with the wide blue strip of water behind us, a smiling happy family. We look at weapons, clothing, jewellery, and relics, amongst which is the *actual* staff of

Moses, used, of course, when he parted the Red Sea. Sam declares the staff a FAKE, and it looks like plastic. No, surely not!

Strategic Photo-Taking

After a sleep-in and a late, leisurely breakfast, the next day we catch the tram from outside our hotel and cross the Galata Bridge to visit the Dolmabahce Palace, the summer residence of the sultans, to check out the extravagant wealth of the Ottoman Empire. Described on the palace website as 'one of the most glamorous places in the world,' we thought it worth seeing.

Walking along the foreshore of the Bosphorus Strait in the sunshine, we arrive at the palace only to find it is closed. The children are not disappointed. I'm not either. It's such a beautiful, bright day. We pose for photos in front of the extraordinary Gate of the Sultan, the entrance to the palace, to show we'd been there.

After only a couple of days away, the constant photo-taking is causing frowny lines to appear on Anthony's face. Usually it's just the four of us on a trip, so I take one, maybe two shots of everyone at a particular place, and he is generally pretty smiley. But now there are three more cameras, so the posing and photo-taking are magnified. At each photo op, there are six to eight photos taken with four different cameras, and that's just a photo of Anthony, the kids, and me, and doesn't include extra photos for 'your eyes were closed' or 'the photo is blurry, let me take another one.'

Anthony's expression becomes more pained as the photos are taken. I realise I need to get the first photo at each place when he's smiling, as by photo four or five, he's lost interest in the whole thing, as has Sam.

And then there's the photos of Mum, me, and Holly, or Maree and David, and also the group photos. By this time, Anthony has wandered off farther along the pretty waterfront esplanade, probably to look for dachshunds.

Shiny Shoes and Happy Souls

Afterwards, the friendliest man in the world approaches and offers to shine Anthony's shoes. He is so insistent that Anthony finally gives in, and then David too. They know what's coming and aren't too bothered when they're hit up for money for something they didn't want in the first place. Mum, Maree, and I find it quite amusing to see the men negotiating with the now adamant man about what a beautiful service he provided and how much it should be worth.

Lots, apparently.

We enjoy a fabulous afternoon in the sunshine, and eat fish and chips by the sparkling blue waters of the strait, watching people, boats, and birds, before heading back to the hotel for our second pack-up of the holiday.

Still no dachshunds spotted.

GALLIPOLI, TURKEY

Date: October 25
Location: Istanbul – Gallipoli – Canakkale
Nights: 1
Dachshunds so far: 0

Peaceful Anzac Cove

Today we leave Istanbul for the long drive out to the Gallipoli Peninsula at the head of the Dardanelles, the strait between two continents where one of the bloodiest battles in recent history occurred. On this four-hour road trip, I play 'Fruit Ninja' with the kids, catch up on the travel blog, and learn about the Gallipoli campaign from Ahmet.

Not only did the battle shape Australian history, but as it was regarded as a great victory for the Ottoman Empire, it also shaped Turkey's. It's all so interesting, and as much as I think I know about the wars Australia has been involved in, once we visit these sites on our holidays, I realise I really don't know much at all.

I didn't know the campaign went on for eight months. I didn't know the war leaders in England took many weeks to call for evacuation even when men were dying of disease and freezing to death as winter snow arrived. I didn't know the campaign was a failure. I didn't know the Allies lost 55 thousand men with another 70 thousand men wounded. I didn't know the Gallipoli campaign came secondary to the battles on the Western Front, so the troops didn't receive as many medical supplies, food, and ammunition as in France, though I'm sure neither battle received what they should have from the powers that be. I didn't know the Allies went into this campaign without any firm battle plan other than—*land on the beaches and beat the Turks*. I may have some of this wrong, but either way I am a little more enlightened.

I hope the kids are enlightened as well. Learning these things in the classroom is one thing, and in fact Sam was studying World War One before we left home, but stepping into trenches and seeing graves and thousands of names on a wall, names of men whose bodies were never found, is a lot for children to take in, but I'm glad they're learning it.

Anthony stands before a grave bearing the name of a young soldier. He stares at the headstone for ages, probably thinking, like me, that Sam is of a similar age. This brings tears to my eyes. I can't even contemplate a parent's misery having to watch their boy go off to war.

I move to the shelter of the trees dotted around Ari Burnu Cemetery. It's quiet and peaceful in Anzac Cove, and there's hardly anyone on the whole peninsula except us. Anthony and the kids step down from the grass of the cemetery to the pebbled beach, and I watch as they skim stones across the water. And of course, even out here there is a stray dog relaxing in the shade.

Ahmet tells us he's been a tour guide on Anzac Day at Gallipoli thirteen times. It's so peaceful here I can't imagine thousands of people milling around. I can't imagine thousands of soldiers and gunfire and death and misery.

But at this moment, on this quiet and serene peninsula, fought over for eight months for its access to the Dardanelles, it's beautiful and calm with only the sounds of water lapping at the shore, sea birds, and the occasional fishing boat chugging past.

The Bitter Taste of War

We load back into the van to wind up the steep hill toward Lone Pine Memorial and Cemetery, the Turkish Memorial, and the Nek. Anthony, the kids, and I step down into trenches still cut into the landscape of the high ridgeline and walk along the places where men fought and died.

The Battle of the Nek was a short, bloody battle, a failure of bad timing, and an attack that should have been called off but wasn't, resulting in hundreds of deaths in mere minutes. The battle was meant to coincide with attacks from other divisions. A wave of Allied soldiers were ordered to attack the Turkish trenches, only twenty-seven metres away. They were met with machine-gun fire and death. Two minutes later another wave of Allies were ordered to advance, and then another—and all met the same fate.

I simply can't imagine the fear the soldiers must have felt, especially having watched the previous waves of men before them and knowing what they were doing was futile. The Battle of the Nek is the closing scene of the movie *Gallipoli* by Peter Weir. Once I hear this, I can *see* it. I can imagine it. I can see Mel Gibson desperately running to tell the commander to stop the next wave but not making it. I know it's only a movie, but the scene is heartbreaking to watch.

We'd wanted to visit Gallipoli for many reasons: to honour our fallen soldiers and to never forget their sacrifices, but also to visit the resting place of my great, great uncle, Private Walter Nelson Jones of the 18th Battalion (infantry). He was killed in action in the last major offensive of the Gallipoli campaign—to capture Hill 60. The first attack on August 21, 1915 gained little ground, and on the twenty-second of August, the inexperienced 18th Battalion was sent in armed only with bayonets. Out of the seven hundred and fifty men of the 18th Battalion, three hundred and eighty three died, including Walter. He presumably died of war wounds (his body was never recovered). He was only twenty-two, and this was his first bitter taste of war after three months of training in Egypt.

Before we left home Mum and I ordered Walter's records from the National Archives. We carry them with us today, and it is a heartbreaking reminder of how difficult it was back then for family at home waiting for news of loved ones. Included in the file are letters from his father, dated in October and November of 1915, asking for news of his son. The records show that in December 1915 Walter is declared wounded and missing. I am sure, in their hearts they knew he had perished, but without news there is always hope. It takes two long years until it is finally ruled in the proceedings of the Court Inquiry held in Rouen, France, that he was 'killed in action.'

We now live in a world of instant connectivity, and we know nearly every minute of every day where our children and loved ones are. How would we cope with not knowing the fate of our child? Not well, I expect.

Private Walter Nelson Jones is remembered in the Lone Pine Memorial looking over the Dardanelles and the Aegean Sea.

Lest we forget.

Seaside Reprieve

The somber mood lifts as we take our seats on the ferry for the twenty-minute trip across to Canakkale for an overnight stop. With the sound of cats meowing—that is, human, cat-like creatures that may have been disguised as Mum and Holly—they serenade us to Canakkale with Maree laughing by their side.

We take a wander around the pretty seaside town of Canakkale, a small village dominated by fishing boats and the huge wicker Trojan horse used in the movie *Troy* with Brad Pitt and Eric Bana.

Not that I was expecting it in Gallipoli or Canakkale, as I don't think they are a sausage dog hangout, but there are still no dachshund sightings.

KUSADASI, TURKEY

Date: *October 26*
Location: *Canakkale – Kusadasi*
Nights: *5*
Dachshunds so far: *0*

Troy, Cats, and a Wooden Horse

I t's a big travel day today, as on the way to Kusadasi, we are visiting the ancient settlements of Troy and Pergamon.

As soon as we arrive in Troy, the kids are delighted to see more cats, a ginormous snail (true story), a few lizards, a big horse made of timber, and—you're not going to believe it—a gift shop. You couldn't ask for a better day, really.

Oh, but hang on, there is an ancient city there too. Nine, in fact. But that's secondary to the fact that we see a dog. And it is no normal dog, but a dog whose bum doesn't touch the ground when it sits. What? Let's *not* listen to our tour guide, so we can examine this strange phenomenon.

'Kids, listen to Ahmet talk about the nine ancient cities of Troy!'

But—dog.

Ahmet shows us around Troy and the layers of the nine cities that archaeologists have uncovered, with foundations being laid, one over the other, over the centuries. The oldest is Troy I, dating back to about 3000 BCE (Before Common Era). Troy VII (about 1300 BCE) was most likely to be related to the stories from Homer (not Simpson). Troy is situated in what was a strategic location in the ancient world—between Asia and Europe, which, I'm guessing, is why this city was rebuilt over and over again in this area.

There are no buildings like in the well-preserved Pompeii, and the ruins are mostly foundations and tumbled-down masonry. If we were wandering without a guide, I don't think we would have had a sense of what Ancient Troy may have looked like, but Ahmet is so knowledgeable it's easy to imagine it as he points out avenues, agoras, foundations, and wells. It's hard to believe that thousands of years of history lie at my feet, as well as a few lazy cats.

While the grandparents stroll around, the kids enjoy climbing into the towering wooden Trojan Horse and looking though the gift shop, the most favourite place in the world for all children on a holiday, especially Holly (and Anthony's least favourite place on a holiday). Anthony waits out front patiently though. That might not last long. It's only been a week and a half. Anything could happen.

Therapy in Pergamon

We continue a couple of hours down the coast of Turkey to Pergamon, a once hilltop fortress in 323 BCE and a thriving city. We don't ascend to the hilltop acropolis as we don't have time, but Ahmet shows us around the Healing Centre of Asclepios, which was similar to a hospital or rehabilitation centre. For sick patrons of the ancient world, there was water therapy, music therapy, psychotherapy, and gymnasiums.

There are tumbled-down columns strewn all about, underground walkways to centuries-old treatment rooms, and cats lazing here and there still soaking up the healing qualities of the centre. Lizards skitter amongst the grass and ruins as Sam jumps from ancient stones and Holly follows cats.

The ruins at Pergamon are a little uneven for achy-kneed oldies, as are most of these sites, Troy included, especially for David, whose knee hasn't quite recovered yet after colliding with a bollard in Istanbul, and Mum, who's had a wonky knee her whole life. But they are coping well with all the walking. I know others at their age would not have kept up, especially with the walking pace Anthony sets!

The Charisma of Kusadasi

After another couple of hours in the van, we wind through the hills to Kusadasi for a five-night stay at the Charisma Hotel. It is one of our splurge hotels, and it's awesome.

Kusadasi sits on the coast of Turkey and the Aegean Sea with beaches and sun and wine—oops I meant—beaches and sun and cats, the native animal of Turkey.

We're all looking forward to some free days to relax with only one half-day tour booked before we get into the busy road travel through Europe, and I'm excited! I really wanted one part of the holiday to be totally relaxing, with time to recharge after the craziness of packing up for the holiday. And with the stress of Coco's death, that last week at home left me exhausted.

At the Charisma, all of our rooms have balconies overlooking the sparkling sea and the setting sun. The oldies are high above in a high-rise room, and I know they love kicking back on their balconies and staring out into the water, especially Mum with her sunset photo-taking obsession.

The hotel buffet has more food than I've ever seen in one place. The tariff includes breakfast and dinner, and we have five days of all-you-can-eat buffets morning and night. We can put on some winter fat before heading off to the cold of Russia. Homer Simpson would have loved it, and we don't mind it either!

The server on the dessert buffet is hilarious. He continuously yells, 'No calorie!' with the biggest grin on his face as he serves up sugar-rich portions of dessert. We are pretty sure this is the only English he knows, as with any attempt to chat to him, his reply is always the same: 'No calorie!'

The first day is filled with swimming, eating, and relaxing on the expansive pool deck at the hotel, and exploring the shops and foreshore of Kusadasi.

World's Most Spectacular Library

Our only tour from Kusadasi is to Ephesus in Selcuk, an ancient Greek city from the tenth century BCE. Similar to Pompeii, the site is still being excavated, and the whole city covers almost two hundred acres, which we probably got to see about a tenth of.

Ephesus is a magnificent connection to the ancient world. As I stand up at the entrance and look down the avenue, bordered by fallen columns with the Library of Celsus rising at the end, it takes my breath away. 'This is so cool' is all I can think.

Once upon a time, before marauding Goths destroyed it in 268 AD, the Temple of Artemis was one of the famed structures here; in fact, it was one of the Seven Ancient Wonders of the World.

The best part of Ephesus for me is the Library of Celsus, completed in 135 AD and the third biggest library of the ancient world, after Alexandria in Egypt and Pergamon. As I stand between the soaring entrance columns, I don't want to leave. I would be happy to sit on the steps of the library a while and read a book or write. Host a Skype book club meeting, perhaps? Built to house over 12 thousand scrolls and as a mausoleum for Celsus, the facade lay in ruins for centuries until restored by archaeologists in the 1970s.

There are also baths, agoras (meeting places), intricately carved columns, capitals, and sarcophaguses. There are temples to Hadrian and Sebastoi and a theatre to seat 24 thousand people, considered to be the largest theatre of the ancient world. I really think Bruce Springsteen should do a concert here. I'll be in the first row hoping he'll pull me up on stage, Courtney-Cox style.

And, there are toilets! Those ancient folks were so clever. They had separate sewage and water pipes, as well as under floor heating for their bathing areas. What happened to civilisation? We went downhill from there, and it took us centuries to get it back.

Holy CATS! They're here in Ephesus, of course. It's Turkey. They dart behind pillars, laze on top of ancient columns in the sun, and perch atop archways, not at all alarmed by the people milling around.

Here's a list I made in my travel blog of our tour of Western Europe in 2009. Sam was eleven and Holly was eight. These were some of their favourite things while on *that* holiday. On this holiday they are fifteen and twelve. Nothing much has changed.

1. *Dogs*
2. *Cats*
3. *Telescopes on bell towers, churches, any lofty monuments*
4. *Lizards*
5. *Parks*
6. *Junky tourist shops*
7. *Pigeons—it is necessary for all pigeons to be chased*
8. *Ice cream*

Hairy Adventures

We soak up the sun in Kusadasi and swim and relax. We play Ping-Pong and mini golf, laugh, watch cruise ships come and go from our balconies, and immerse ourselves in the Aegean Sea out the front of our hotel, as does the yellow Rotary rubber ducky. We also dodge cats, and the kids video cats and kittens doing cat-like things. There are many walks down to the small town to explore and shop, and for David, a visit to the barber.

This is an adventure. He sees a barbershop advertising haircuts for two liras which he likes the sounds of, the smaller the number the better, according to David. A smiling barber seats him quickly and begins to cut away at David's hair. Chairs are brought outside for Mum and Maree, along with a small table with Turkish tea and biscuits. Anthony and I pass them and with a wave continue our shopping. It is later back at the hotel that we hear the story of David's epic haircut, told by Mum and Maree.

They show pictures of David not only getting a very lengthy haircut, but a facial and face massage, a shave, and an eyebrow, nose, and ear hair trim.

'Maree and I are sitting there enjoying our tea,' Mum tells us, 'and at first we're thinking: how good is this for two liras? They keep asking David if he wants this and that, and he keeps saying yes. And then after a while, we start to wonder how much this will end up costing.'

David grins at the camera in the photos, happy with his cheap barbershop visit and is told by the smiling barber that he looks ten years younger. Minutes later when told the price, an argument starts and all the extras are pointed out to David, including the tea and biscuits for Mum and Maree. David is still resistant, but when two other men appear from the back of the barbershop, he decides to pay up.

'How much was it?' I ask.

'Eighty euros!' gasps Maree.

'No way!' I exclaim. I can't help but start to laugh.

'Maree and I laughed all the way back,' adds Mum, 'but David doesn't think it's funny at all.'

No he probably doesn't. I look online and find story after story of barbershop shenanigans in Turkey, how some barbers prey on tourists by acting as though all they are providing is included in the price. He's been had! I can understand why David is cranky.

Later in the day Holly and Mum decide they want to return to the town on their own for some shopping.

And don't they have a story to tell upon their return a couple of hours later. After hopping on the bus out the front of the hotel, they miss the stop where they should have gotten off. They hop off at the next stop, thinking it will be all right, but it's not. They have no idea where they are and decide to walk down a road, which leads them to dark, narrow streets with lots of men in groups. Not long after they find themselves walking beside a creepy cemetery. Nothing looks familiar. More than half an hour later, they finally come across some buses. No one speaks English, but Mum has her room card from the hotel, which she shows to a bus driver, and he points them in the right direction. I don't think they'll do that again!

Vinegar and Cat Pee

We set sail on a lavish sunset cruise on the second to last day, it is so-o-o-o- luxurious . . . and the wine ever so delightful! We stretch out on the deck with cocktails and soak up the sun in our bikinis and speedos. Do you detect sarcasm? OK, it's time to come clean.

The cruise costs five Turkish lira per person (about 2.50 AUD), on a slightly rickety boat, with dirty beanbags on the upper deck and slightly bitter wine that has accents of vinegar and cat pee, in large glasses that look none too clean. Mum and I still have a few sips, but we can't quite polish off the buckets of wine we are served. I get the heebie-jeebies when a pre-worn scarf is put on my head in a mosque in Istanbul, but serve me vinegar, cat-pee wine in a dirty glass, and I'll give it a go. Go figure.

So it wasn't luxurious but so lovely all the same. Who needs luxury? (Says the girl with 300 dollar suede fashion hiking boots she bought for the holiday because she saw Sarah Jessica Parker wearing them in a magazine). The sunset is one of the most beautiful I've seen with the colours reflecting on the water. We snap photo after photo as the sun sinks into the ocean. We snuggle, laugh, and photo bomb each other while we watch Turkey's coastline slip past.

Although the weather is nice, it's late in the season and light jackets are needed, but we all enjoy these last moments of warmer weather. I want to stay longer, explore more of Turkey and the Greek Islands. But it's time to squash down summer clothes in vacuum bags and say bye-bye to the warm weather.

Watching the sunset on our last swimming day, I snap photos of the kids with the camera facing towards the sunset, turning the forms of their bodies to black shadows. They reach to touch fingertips like the image of God and Adam in the Sistine Chapel, making what is one of my favourite photos of the holiday.

I have come to the conclusion there are no dachshunds in Turkey. The cats have scared them all off.

Holiday dachshund spotting competition. Zero.

Russia, here we come!

6

MOSCOW, RUSSIA

Date: *October 31*
Location: *Kusadasi – Moscow*
Nights: *4*
Dachshunds so far: *0*

Dachshund Spotting, Game-On!

After a long travel day from Kusadasi, we finally arrive in Moscow just as night is falling. When our driver meets us, I breathe a sigh of relief. Russia is the only destination I'm most unsure of. I know tourists travel here, this isn't something new, but one of the downsides of travelling to Russia in November is that tour companies no longer operate group tours. We are on a tour I designed myself with no official tour operators guiding us, only individual city guides and transport between each place.

The traffic into Moscow is heavy, creeping slowly along, giving us plenty of time to gaze out the windows of the van. I see a white church with gleaming, gold, onion-shaped domes catching the last light of the day as it breaks through the clouds. A thrill goes through me. Never in my wildest dreams as a teenager, or even after

Anthony and I were married, did I think I'd be able to travel the world. With a mortgage and kids and determined to pay off debts, overseas travel was out of the question for us for many years. But now, here we are in Russia. I'm excited, especially when . . . wait for it . . .

There's a dachshund spotted by Anthony, and finally the holiday dachshund-spotting competition begins on the congested road into Moscow. And not just one dachshund, but two! A tan one, and a black and tan one, both in winter coats and both of the miniature, smooth haired variety.

I'm positive the poor driver has no idea what's going on with the sudden eruption of glee in the van. Seven Westerners suddenly shouting, laughing, and pointing.

We always keep an eye out for dachshunds on our trips, but unfortunately for the rest of us, historically Anthony always spots them first. Plus, he is pretty good at gloating about it and refers to himself as the King of Dachshund Spotting.

Dachshund Spotting Total:
Anthony 2

The sight of the two dachshunds, so similar to Coco and Charlie, being led through a park stirs up so many emotions. First, excitement, and then sudden, and quite unexpected, sadness and tears. Especially for Holly and me. The boys are stoic, but I know the sighting has stirred up their grief as well.

'Why did Coco have to die?' is a common question Holly asks, and oftentimes it leads to my dad as well, 'Why did Pa have to die?'

These are questions I cannot answer. Holly and I hug and talk of all the dachshunds we're going to spot.

And then, only minutes later, Holly spots a black dachshund in a park by the road. More excitement in the van ensues. I'm sure the driver can't wait to drop us off.

Dachshund Spotting Total:
Anthony 2, Holly 1

'We'll beat Daddy,' Holly and I declare.

Anthony gives a cheeky smile, shakes his head, and taps his chest, responding, 'I'm the King of Dachshund Spotting.'

'Na-a-a-h!' is all we can come up with. Not a great comeback, I know.

'It was so funny how Coco would hide under the pillows on your bed when the vacuum was on,' Holly remarks.

'It was.' Thinking of it brings tears to my eyes again. The instant the vacuum was turned on we always knew where to find her: snuggled underneath the fancy throw pillows on our bed. 'Remember the time we put the faux fur wrap around her neck, and she sat there like a princess amongst the pillows?'

Holly grins. 'And what about the time she got under the fence and chased the donkey next door?'

I laugh at this, loud enough for the driver to glance at me. What a nightmare that was—trying to persuade Coco to come home without getting too close to the cranky donkey. Charlie, the better-behaved dog of the two, came as soon as we called him, but not Coco. She was a fairly stubborn dog. A normal dachshund.

I remember how, every time, she'd walk the whole length of the house to come and see me when I was in the bath. I'd hear the click of her claws on the tiles and her head would pop up over the side of the bath for a pat. And always, when I walked back into the bedroom, she would be laying on the soft throw rug on the end of the bed, waiting for me. I am going to miss her.

We arrive at the hotel, but before we head out into the streets of Moscow, big jackets, warm hats, and gloves are required for the now four-degree Celsius weather we've descended into. The coast of Turkey and its sunshine are a long way from here.

A Cow in Moscow?

There aren't any restaurants near our hotel, and we're getting hungrier by the minute, especially the teenage boy of the group, and it's after 8 pm. We walk for half an hour, almost all the way to Red Square, passing beautifully lit buildings and weirdly, a person in a black-and-white cow suit handing out balloons. We cross busy roads that aren't meant to be crossed. Not by tourists. Not by anyone. David is almost clipped by a car.

On the way back, we realise there are pedestrian tunnels under the road, but we silly tourists, oh no, we brave the busy road between cars, which is OK for Anthony, the kids, and me, but not so achievable for Mum, Maree, and David.

All we find for dinner is a Starbucks, but we're looking for more than coffee and a chocolate brownie. I want hearty Russian food on our first night in Moscow, like . . . I realise I have no idea what Russian food is, but I know I don't want Starbucks!

Even during this desperate quest for real food, Holly corners me to play her clapping game, but the process of thinking of boys' and girls' names has become a bit boring. I suggest that at each clap one must say a place we've been to or visited on the trip, and the game starts anew. This is way more fun! Mum, Maree, and David join in for a turn each, and their voices ring out with all the places we've seen so far until one of them mucks it up, repeats a place, or flounders when it's their turn. And it starts all over again.

After a long walk, we end up back where we started, at the hotel's expansive bar for dinner, which would have been awesome had there been Russian food on the menu. But no, the Marriott Grand Moscow has hamburgers, chips, and club sandwiches. They have wine though, so I'm appeased. I'd been told Russia was expensive, and after the 30 Australian dollar hamburger, I'm determined to find a local restaurant for further meals.

The following day we receive a recommendation for a tasty, reasonably priced restaurant from a tour guide. The restaurant is called 'My My' (pronounced 'moo moo'), and we had already passed it on our walk but didn't realise what it was. Ah, the cow handing out balloons—now it all makes sense.

Onion Domes and Pineapple Swirls

At 10 am we meet Tatiana in the hotel foyer for our half-day tour of Moscow. First up—the iconic Red Square. It is large, seventy by three hundred metres, and surrounded by the vibrant red brick ramparts of the Kremlin, the stepped red and black granite building housing Lenin's tomb, GUM shopping arcade, the castle-like State Historical Museum, and the iconic Saint Basil's Cathedral. Tatiana informs us that Lenin's Mausoleum is closed, but I'm not sure I want to see his pasty, embalmed body anyway. In fact, I'm absolutely positive I don't want to see it.

The square is crowded with tourists and school children. We turn in circles taking in all the buildings, but of course what commands our attention is Saint Basil's Cathedral with its brightly coloured onion-shaped domes. One dome has a green and bronze swirl; another is a yellow and green diagonal pattern, almost pineapple-like in appearance. There is a dark green and red dome, and a circus tent-like blue and white swirl above rows of scalloping and diagonal patterns over the deep red base of the main building.

It is a jumble of colour, breathtaking in design, and one of those buildings so recognisable to a particular city. Saint Basil's means Moscow, like Big Ben means London, or the Eiffel Tower is Paris.

Now a museum, Saint Basil's Cathedral, built in the sixteenth century under the reign of Ivan the Terrible, who Tatiana tells us wasn't so terrible, has a total of nine chapels with eight side-churches around the central church. By the way, don't quote me with Ivan's 'un-terrible' status. That's Tatiana's call, not mine!

Afterwards we're driven around Moscow to see more of the city's buildings, like the Bolshoi Theatre, old KGB headquarters, statues of Alexander Pushkin, Lenin, and Stalin, and a towering monument to the Conquerors of Space, followed by a stop at Sparrow Hills, the highest point in the city, to take in the view over Moscow. It is a dreary day, so the view isn't overly exciting. It is a sprawl of grey on this grey day, with the high-rise buildings towering over the curve of the Moskva River.

After the tour when Anthony, Sam, and David go for a walk, Anthony spots another dachshund. We hound Anthony (dachshund-style, ha-ha!) when they arrive back from their walk.

Q: Did you pat it?
A: No.

Q: Did you get a photo?
A: No.

Q: What colour?
A: Black.

Q: Was it a miniature?
A: Yes.

Q: Was it a smooth, longhair, or wirehair?
A: Smooth.

Dachshund Spotting Total:
Anthony 3, Holly 1

On our previous trip to Europe, we saw four dachshunds, the entire time, and within two days of arriving to Moscow, four have been spotted already! I wonder how many we're going to see on the trip and how many types. I remember the first time we saw a standard dachshund at a dog show. I was astounded by its size. It was probably twice the size of our miniature dachshunds, with a deeper chest, longer neck, and simply bigger all over.

Holly is looking at pictures of Coco and Charlie on her iPad. They are play fighting with bared teeth and crazy eyes. Without looking up, she asks, 'Dad's going to win the competition, isn't he?'

'No,' I say at the same time that Anthony says, 'Yes,' with a big grin.

My My, How Delicious

We all meet in the hotel bar for pre-dinner drinks and card games while being interviewed by Maree on her video camera about our favourite parts of the day. Soon we are wandering down to visit the fat cow for dinner at My My. We are pretty happy to pay the equivalent of 40 Australian dollars for all seven of us to eat. I think Mum's costs five dollars, and Maree and David's is ten. Do the maths, people! It's a bargain!

Set up like a cafeteria, we grab trays, slide them along the rails, and point to what we want with vague, single word, stunted English. Meat, point finger. Potato, point finger. Mumble and point to unknown dish that looks edible. The tables upstairs are filled, so we file downstairs to what looks like a German beer hall, with long tables, bench seats, dark timber, and a slightly uneven flagstone floor.

Our meal of chicken soup, brown rice, and a goulash-looking stew is hearty, warm, and tasty. And it's Russian. I'm sure a regular traveller to Moscow would be horrified, and somewhere there is a street of fine dining to sample the most delectable Russian cuisine, but this is just what we are looking for.

Missing Dad

As David sips his beer, tucks into goulash, and chats to Anthony, I can't help but think how much I want my own dad here. I miss him, and I know it's playing on Mum's mind too. My dad would have loved this holiday; this man who declared for years that caravanning was the only holiday worth doing. Then on a trip to Europe he and Mum guided themselves through Italy, France, and Germany, and they had a ball. They got lost, Dad chatted to everyone he met, and they saw what could only be described as a man-poodle, but most of all they had fun, so Mum began to plan their next trip overseas. But he never made it. Within five months of returning home, he died. I wish things were different, but I'm so fortunate to have David here with us. He's pretty good at the old dad cuddle that I think all daughters need, no matter their age.

Anthony wants to go for a nighttime walk down to Red Square, but I don't join him although I love our walks on our own when we are travelling. But because I'd somehow damaged my foot in Kusadasi, whiney noises are coming out of my mouth. To save Anthony from my moaning, I thought I should stay in and rest up, drink a glass of wine, and write the next entry of my travel blog.

Anthony sets out on his own, which just quietly, I think he is happy about. He can stroll at his own pace, which is lightening-fast, Olympic walker speed but without the lock knee and bum wiggle. It's a manly focused stride, with eyes peeled for wandering dachshunds and his destination of Red Square firmly set in his mind. Nothing will deter him from his path. Nothing!

Anthony returns from his speed walk to Red Square delighted with his find. 'You should have come,' he declares. Apparently, Red Square at night is spectacular. I Google it and instantly regret my decision not to go.

Hail Mary

After sampling the fabulous breakfasts at the Marriott Grand and nicking our muffin and fruit morning tea under serviettes, we meet Tatiana again for our tour around the Moscow metro stations. It doesn't sound too exciting, does it? But many of the stations are beautiful and worth a look.

Opened in 1935, it's one of the busiest metro systems in the world. The stations are deep below the streets of Moscow, the deepest at seventy-four metres. We descend into the depths on steep and seemingly never-ending escalators that take Maree, who doesn't like escalators *or* heights, ten repeated Hail Marys to get down. She grips David's arm tightly and does not let go until we reach the bottom.

Every station shows an ornate display of extravagance, looking more like luxurious hotel foyers instead of train stations. The platforms are decorated with vibrant mosaics, paintings, statues, polished granite, stained glass panels, and chandeliers. After taking numerous photos, we join commuters on train after train on short trips all around the city. Holly poses, holding the Rotary rubber ducky aloft inside Komsomolskaya Metro Station, as does our guide Tatiana, who grins widely as she holds the small yellow duck in her hand.

Afterwards, we visit the Arbat, an area of Moscow dating back to the fifteenth century. We stroll along Arbat Street where nobility, artists, writers, and professors once lived. It is now a shopping district lined with many shops, from tacky souvenir shops to fine Russian arts and crafts, pottery, and jewellery stores.

Tatiana takes us to one of the better souvenir shops (or so we thought). I buy a nine-piece babushka doll set for way too much money, Christmas tree decorations, and two porcelain dachshund figurines, one brown and one black, like Coco and Charlie, again for too much money—although I feel any dachshund purchase is a necessary item, like food and shelter and wine. Anthony may not agree with this statement.

As Mum was the one who spotted the two dachshund figurines first, she thinks she should be credited with a dachshund sighting. Anthony denies it swiftly.

We find out, a full year later, that Mum's equally expensive Christmas-inspired babushka doll set has just the Santa. No Mrs. Santa inside, no Christmas tree or Snowman lying in wait inside Santa's ample belly, rolling around like a bowl full of jelly. Nothing inside. Ripped off!

For dinner, in keeping with our search for authentic Russian food, we go to the Bud Diner. What? Anthony felt like a hamburger, so we have a night of burgers, beer, ribs, and chips.

Then, as if we haven't walked enough today, we set off for our big walk down to Red Square. Red Square looks spectacular. It is lit up like a Christmas tree, with lights lining the roofline and windows of the GUM shopping arcade and the State Historical Museum. The red star on top of each tower of the Kremlin shines brightly, as does Saint Basil's Cathedral, which almost looks like a Technicolor vision at night.

The Gremlin

On our last day in Moscow, we visit the Kremlin. Holly later admits she thought it was called the Gremlin and is blaming Tatiana's accent. We follow Tatiana up the sloped walkway through drizzling rain to the arched tunnel of the Kremlin's main entrance.

It's not at all like what I thought it would be. I thought it would be dark and dreary and KGB-like. But it isn't. It's open and airy with green lawns and lovely buildings. We see where the president stays when he visits and the soldiers' barracks, as well as the parliament and the Tsar Cannon and Tsar Bell, the biggest cannon and bell in the whole entire world.

We thought we'd finish off our stay with a visit to the Moscow Circus, but when we'd tried to get tickets for the evening show, it was sold out. We mention it to Tatiana, and with a wink she says she 'knows a guy.' Twenty minutes later in the grounds of the Kremlin, her big, burly Russian guy, who does not speak English, approaches. Trusting Tatiana we make the transaction of rubles for circus tickets, and he quickly disappears. Have we been ripped off? Who knows! But we're going to the circus!

The circus is great, of course, so I'm glad we managed to get the tickets. Going to the circus in Moscow is a pretty nice treat. There are the funniest of clowns and a spectacularly top-hatted and mustachioed ringmaster. Acrobats, trapeze artists, and jugglers dazzle us, as well as a ballerina walking a tightrope, horses, tigers, seals, panthers, and more.

When we return to the hotel, there's a message from Angela at home with a picture of Charlie on her lap on the lounge. He looks as happy as a pig in mud. Angela smiles wryly in the photo. Her own dogs are not allowed on the lounge, but somehow Charlie has convinced her it's a good idea. Smart boy.

ST. PETERSBURG, RUSSIA

Date: November 4
Location: Moscow – St. Petersburg
Nights: 4
Dachshunds: 4

For the Love of Children

After a five-hour train journey playing cards and games, and a drunk man who tripped over onto Maree, which gave her a bit of a scare, we arrive in St. Petersburg, aka the Venice of the North, named for its canals and waterways. There isn't a lot to see out the window on the way, only the signs of winter with stark trees, small plots of land, even smaller houses, and untidy towns that are more than a little worse for wear.

I like seeing our name on a card when we arrive somewhere, and sure enough, there's our driver standing at the end of the train platform. On the way to our hotel, we drive down Nevsky Prospeckt, the long, broad shopping avenue of St. Petersburg. The lights and buildings look so beautiful lit up at night, and I can't wait to see more on our tours. Maree is particularly excited. She has always wanted to visit St. Petersburg and never thought she'd have the chance. As I glance out the window, I notice there are signs in English here and there, unlike Moscow, which was not particularly tourist-friendly with signs.

The enormous Saint Isaac's Cathedral borders our hotel on Saint Isaac's Square. It is a stunning view to take in from the hotel. We quickly settle in, and as it's late already, we go to the hotel restaurant for dinner. No luck there with any Russian cuisine, but the Italian restaurant satisfies the pizza-loving Sam.

There are no major issues, but I realise Anthony and I need more one-on-one time with the kids. Walks, dinners, whatever, but *more* of it. We travelled for three months with the kids before, and I remember our dinners and walks being full of wonderful chats about the day and listening to the children's funny comments and observations. But with five adults at the table, this is not happening as much. At a dinner, five adults can dominate a conversation, and I find myself switching between the two groups, from adults back to kids and back again. Even though Sam and Holly are not being left out—they *are* included by everyone—it's not quite the same as two parents chatting directly to their children.

As soon as we get back to our hotel room, I talk to Anthony about it, and he agrees. We love our parents, and they love us, but we also have our little family unit of the four of us, and we need to make sure we have special time together.

Winter Coats and All

This morning it is cold, wet, and drizzly. *B-r-r-r.* We've definitely hit the cold part of the journey, and the thermals and warmer clothes are out to stay. Being 650 kilometres north of Moscow and not far from Finland, there is a chill in the air. We are in cold territory here! And it's *so* dark! We go down to breakfast at 9:00 am, and it doesn't start to lighten until around 9:30 am.

Helen, our tour guide, meets us in the foyer of the hotel, and soon we are cruising the streets of the city. But wait! We have a startling event on the way to the first tourist stop, an event that puts winning the dachshund-spotting competition farther out of reach—for some of us. Anthony spots *three* dachshunds. THREE, people! What on earth is going on? Why couldn't I have seen them first?

We gaze through the van window, our attention immediately ripped from Helen, as she tells us about the Nazi assault on St. Petersburg in World War Two, to watch as three of the cutest dachshunds in winter coats trot through a park, sniffing and wagging their tails. Eventually the doggies are out of sight, and we sit back to remark on this wondrous event (the dachshunds, not the history lesson).

Dachshund Spotting Total:
Anthony 6, Holly 1

I am stating the obvious, I know, but Anthony insists I record this: the rest of us have seen ZERO dachshunds. He and Holly are currently the only worthy opponents in this competition. Sam says he's not looking for dachshunds anyway, but David, not believing this *at all*, laughs at Sam's bold declaration.

With a smile Helen advises us dachshunds are *very* popular dogs in Russia, so all of us are determined to keep our eyes peeled for sausage-like creatures with short legs. Some heckling ensues about beating Anthony, who merely smiles and shakes his head confidently, his eyes on the surrounding parks and pathways. And while we're all chatting about how we are going to beat him, I realise we are *not watching*. Ha! Anthony has this in the bag.

History Lessons with Helen

Helen continues to tell us of the siege of Leningrad (the former St. Petersburg), the military blockade by the German army. The siege began in September 1941 and ended 872 days later. Hitler, having already planned to raze the city, had no intention of maintaining its population. Helen tells stories of starvation, of people eating bread made of ashes, of desperation and cannibalism and the resulting deaths of hundreds of thousands of people. What happened here was horrific and is regarded as one of the most destructive sieges in history. No matter what leaders of countries commit to within these catastrophic wars, the normal citizens pay such a terrible price.

It is a grey day with a bitterly cold breeze carrying light rain with it. We prepare for the cold with beanies, gloves, and scarves, and exit the van to visit the Peter and Paul Cathedral, a Russian Orthodox Church, which contains the burial vault of the Romanov dynasty. It is chilly wandering around in the rain, and we are glad to pop into the church for a bit of warmth.

Russia has such an interesting history—brothers murdering brothers to obtain the throne, wives murdering husbands, and fathers murdering sons—such a friendly bunch! It is fascinating listening to Helen as she tells of the lead up to the Russian Revolution and the assassination of the Romanovs in October 1918. The revolution dismantled the autocracy and led to the rise of the Soviet Union.

The Romanovs had ruled for three centuries before they were executed, but the bodies of two of the children, Anastasia and Alexei, were never found, leading some to believe they were still alive. In 1991 that mystery was solved when bodies were exhumed from a pit nineteen kilometres out of the city. Interestingly, Helen tells us that Prince Phillip, Duke of Edinburgh, who is a distant descendant, supplied his DNA to confirm the identity of the Romanovs. After decades they were finally laid to rest in the Romanov burial vault.

When the tour finishes, we're all in need of a warm, hearty meal after the cold and rain and murdering Russians, so we go to the first restaurant we can find near our hotel that isn't ridiculously expensive. We find one that has Russian fare although the entire restaurant is French influenced. I learn later that the origins of stroganoff, a favourite Aussie meal, are French. We feast on pasta, soups, stroganoff, and cups of tea and hot chocolate to warm our bones. This has been our first day of miserable weather, but it is of no consequence. We are on holiday! Who cares? Not us!

A Possible BFF

Today's tour is to the Hermitage Museum, a group of buildings that includes the Winter Palace, the former home of the tsars. Catherine the Great finished the building in 1837 and began her extensive art collection. The palace is so opulent it's hard to get my mind around the fact that people actually lived here. It's like wandering through the Vatican in Rome. The palace is so large, it crosses over canals, and boats can be seen drifting underneath. We're only doing a half-day tour, but true art connoisseurs could have spent the whole day. Children perhaps need only twenty minutes in the gift shop!

I'm no art aficionado, but the museum is truly amazing. We see paintings by Renoir, Rembrandt, Monet, Cezanne, Degas, Leonardo da Vinci, Rafael, a sculpture by Michelangelo, and the most amazingly detailed mosaics. There is also a collection of Egyptian antiquities, jewellery, and sculptures. The centerpiece of one of the halls is the two hundred-year-old Peacock Clock, a timepiece and automaton with three golden mechanical birds, an owl, a peacock and a rooster, housed in a huge glass case.

A lady tries to join our private tour. At first I think she is merely *extremely* interested in the exact same paintings as us, but then it becomes obvious. Anthony tells me not to worry, but when she starts standing in front of me and then Mum, we can't even see the artwork our guide is telling us about. I decide to say something, but she doesn't speak English, so I don't know how she understands what our guide is saying.

I am all for sharing. If she had hung at the back and not intruded, it would have been fine and dandy, but we didn't pay for a private tour for our family to have someone start pushing in front of us and blocking our view. She understood my firmly spoken but polite, 'Go away,' though. Rant over.

In the evening Anthony, the kids, and I walk along Nevsky Prospeckt to do some shopping, and I drag the family into the House of Books, a large bookshop in a beautiful, old art nouveau style building. In there I'm determined to find a copy of Australian author Kate Forsyth's book *The Wild Girl*, which has just been released in Russia. I decide I'll be Kate's best friend forever if from a bookshop in St. Petersburg in Russia, I tweet a picture of me with her Russian print book. No such luck though. They don't have it, even though I came prepared with its Russian name and everything, so I miss my chance to become Kate's BFF.

More Duck Down, Please

The weather is changing, becoming colder every day, and at one or two degrees Celsius new jackets are required. After going into several shops, Holly now has a new duck down jacket, a longer and warmer one.

Because of the colder temperatures, I need an extra layer under the jacket I have, but as it is too tight, I need a new jacket too. I'm so fussy with jackets though, and I can't find one I like. It all comes down to the hood. Hats, beanies, and hoods—they don't look good on me. However, instead of coming to terms with this terrible calamity and moving on, I defer the jacket purchase, choosing to remain cold and commenting on my coldness to anyone who will listen.

Anthony and I have dinner with the kids this evening, our first with them, and it's fabulous. Russian fare? No, we go to an Italian restaurant for dinner where Sam eats a margherita pizza for the third night in a row. It's so nice to have this one-on-one with the kids over a meal, and even though it's only been a couple of weeks away, I've definitely missed this. 'Isn't this nice?' I ask. 'Yes, Mum,' the kids obediently respond.

On our way back, we spy Mum, Maree, and David enjoying a meal at Garcon, the French restaurant where we ate the day before. We peek through the window but can't get their attention. They are chatting and laughing and having a great time without us. As we wander back to the hotel, I think again about the wonderful friendship that's forming between the three of them, a friendship beyond being Anthony's parents and mine.

The Golden Dome

After a welcome sleep-in for all and a late breakfast, we have the last day to ourselves. We decide to visit the enormous Saint Isaac's Cathedral and its shining gold dome. The cathedral is the largest Russian Orthodox cathedral in the city and the fourth largest basilica (by the volume under the cupola) in the world, so you can imagine how big it is.

The cathedral's main dome, plated with pure gold, rises 101.5 metres from the ground. Inside, the church is decorated with icons, paintings, statues, and soaring columns of green malachite. It is impressive, to say the least, and I proceed to take a gazillion photos.

There are three hundred stairs to the top of the cathedral, with what I think are specially made seats on the way up for Mum, Maree, and David to have a pit stop. I'm pretty impressed by the amount of walking they're doing, especially with dodgy knees, hips, and backs. We are generally walking at least ten to fifteen kilometres a day, and some days even more but they are managing well, as long as there are some seats along the way or a cup of coffee.

Maree, David, and Mum catch up to us at the top, and we gaze over St. Petersburg. It's a cloudy day, but no rain thankfully. There is something wonderful about being high over a town and peering around. It gives me a sense of where everything is. There is always some type of 'aha' moment for me when I climb a tower or church dome, as in, 'Oh, so the river is over there.'

Across the city, the lofty golden spire of the St. Peter and Paul Cathedral gleams brightly, stark against the grey-sky day, so bright it almost seems artificially lit. Rising 123 metres, the spire has an angel at the top holding a cross. I recall Helen telling us the day before that no building in St. Petersburg is allowed to be higher than this spire. Looking over the city, I notice that there are no high-rise buildings, and it's quite lovely really.

Saint Isaac's Cathedral is so big it takes up a whole block. On the way out, our group is separated, so we circle the block looking for each other. How we managed to do that is baffling, but thankfully with our hotel across the street, there is no chance of anyone becoming lost. Just to be clear, so there is no confusion, the Master of the Map, Anthony, would never be lost.

We then embark on our one-hour canal cruise along the waterways of historic St. Petersburg, although in the hour we'll only see a small portion of St. Petersburg's seventy rivers and canals and six hundred bridges.

The boat's top deck, and our heads, are very close to the underside of some of the bridges, but we safely sail underneath and past the eighteenth century Strogonov Palace, once owned by the Counts and Barons of Strogonov, after whom the dish was named. We really enjoy seeing St. Petersburg from a different perspective while cruising past the architectural stunners St. Petersburg has to offer. Palaces, churches, and monuments slip by as we cruise down canal after canal and finally out onto the choppier and very wide Neva River. It's so cold that Holly, Mum, Maree, and I snuggle together against the cool breeze. I suspect the cruises won't run for much longer, and for these shivering Australians, we are glad of the blankets they hand out to everyone.

Beanie Bothers

After a bakery lunch of pastries and fresh rolls, the girls go shopping. I have a beanie situation that needs rectifying before I drive Anthony crazy. Since we arrived in the cold weather, I've moaned, 'This beanie is itching my forehead,' even more times than 'These pretzels are making me thirsty.' True story.

Don't judge me, I have a sensitive forehead. After trying on about twenty beanies, I purchase one with a non-scratchy polar fleece lining.

Mum buys a new beanie too, as she is having some beanie-pushing-her-glasses-down-her-nose issues. Holly requires a new one, as the ginormous pom-pom on the top of current beanie is so big she can't pull the hood of her new jacket up over her head. And they mess your hair up! Well, Mum's, Maree's, and my hair anyway. Holly says her hair is awesome. Who would have thought beanies could be so bothersome? I must point out that the boys do not have any beanie issues. David's hair is almost never messed up. Neither is Anthony's nor Sam's.

You are now all up to date with the beanie situation.

The Wonders of Quality Time

Mum and I head to the bar for pre-dinner drinks and manage to squeeze in two wines before everyone else arrives for dinner. There is something so nice about holiday drinks and dinners, and about having no other agenda except to enjoy the holiday and the company of your travel companions. At home there are constant jobs to do, work, school, and never-ending things to stop you spending quality time with family. 'Isn't this nice?' pops out of my mouth yet again, to which I force the kids and Anthony to reply. They nod as though appeasing a nutter. But it *is* nice.

We enjoy a fabulous Russian meal of beef dumplings with sour cream and dill, beef stroganoff, chicken schnitzel, and pizza. You'll never guess who picked pizza.

Anthony and I go for a big walk after dinner along the Neva River. We love the brisk air and travelling in the early winter. I'm not sure I'd like to be here in February, but as long as it's not raining too much, we reckon this is the best time to travel. We've been lucky so far with only one day of rain, but some snow would be exciting! I've already been searching the weather websites to see if snow is expected. I switch between websites until I find the one that tells me what I want to hear. Will there be snow? I hope so—in Estonia at least!

(8)

TALLINN, ESTONIA

Date: November 8
Location: St. Petersburg – Tallinn
Nights: 1
Dachshunds so far: 7

Nothing a Sharp Yank Won't Fix . . .

Our van arrives for the transfer from St. Petersburg to Tallinn in Estonia. Two burly men with limited English jump out to help us with our bags. They are brusque but friendly enough. We set off and minutes later, on the way out of St. Petersburg, Anthony spots a brown miniature dachshund trotting along with its owner. Shrieking and pointing follow, to the confusion of the drivers.

Dachshund Spotting Total:
Anthony 7, Holly 1

It's raining and isn't a great day to be on the roads, especially as the road between St. Petersburg and Estonia is terrible and not marked well. The edges are broken, uneven, and lined with gravel and mud. It is not a steady or comfortable drive, but an on-the-edge-of-your-seat kind of drive where the person at the wheel struggles to keep the car in the lane.

Minutes later the car swerves off the road and into the mud. The driver loses control but manages to right the vehicle with a sharp yank at the wheel, and we jerk back onto the road. The two drivers sit stony-faced, and the man in the passenger seat barks a few words to the other. David was watching and swears the man went to sleep. He calls out to them asking what the problem is, but all we are given is a shrug and wave.

All are quiet in the car, my heart is thumping in my chest, and it's at this point I wonder why I decided to book road transport between Russia and Estonia. I must have lost my mind. Initially, I was pilfering travel ideas from a Russian tour company that doesn't operate at this time of year, and as *they* transfer their guests via private van, I thought I'd do the same.

But now I'm regretting it. We could have had a perfectly nice plane trip without all this stony-faced hassle. We're in the dreary, broken-down outskirts of St. Petersburg in between Russian and Estonia, two countries that are not the friendliest of neighbours, with two brusque drivers who don't speak English. And it gets worse.

Ex-Soviet Bureaucratic Joys

The checkpoint between Russia and Estonia is a long procession of inspections. First we pull over at a random stop on the side of the road in the middle of nowhere. A guard, stomping into the van, brusquely demands our passports, and all are quiet as he studies them carefully, one by one. Not long after, we pull into what looks like a petrol station. The driver gets out, produces some paperwork to a guard, and points to us inside the van. The guard merely nods but doesn't take the papers. Twenty minutes later, the driver is still standing there with the paperwork clutched in his hand. Eventually another guard steps onto the van and checks our passports. Another ten minutes pass, and finally the driver signals that we are to go into the building.

When we get off the van, I'm a little tense and not happy when we're told we have to go in, one by one, to the cranky-faced lady at the desk to have our passports stamped. I think I should be able to stay with the children, but we're not allowed. I can still see them, but I'm not happy.

After a visit to absolutely filthy toilets, we see sniffer dogs led onto the van by strong-armed guards while other guards look over the bus, inside and out with torches. Finally we are allowed back on, and we depart—but it's not over yet!

A few minutes later, when we think it's all done and dusted, the van pulls onto the side of the road again, and a tall, uniformed guard hops on to check Anthony's, the kids', Mum's, and my passports. He doesn't bother with Maree's and David's. I figure they must look trustworthy. It might have been a good time to ask the guard to pose with the Rotary rubber ducky. Hmm, maybe not.

And it still isn't finished—still one more checkpoint—I wonder if we're *ever* going to get out of there. Before too long though, I realise all the stops so far were to leave Russia, and this checkpoint is to obtain entry to Estonia. And the line of cars is huge. Now I understand why the four hundred-kilometre drive was listed as taking seven hours. After all the hassle, I'm glad to be out of Russia and on our way, and I'm *still* wondering why I didn't book flights.

The passing landscape is dreary and depressing. A lot of the buildings are un-kept and rundown, and I'm again reminded of how lucky we are to live in Australia. Estonia's countryside is quite bleak with rundown, tiny houses clustered around communal gardens. There don't seem to be any shops or facilities near these houses.

Sausage-Dog Envy

About half an hour over the border into Estonia, we drive through a small town, and with a burst of noise in the van, David yells, 'DACHSHUND!' We all turn to see a tan dachshund prancing along in a small park by the road with owner in tow. David's face is split with the widest smile. It's his first dachshund sighting, and he is jubilant. Minutes later there is another dachshund call from Anthony, and again, the usual eruption of:

'Dachshund!'

'Where?'

'Next to the building/in the park/on the other side of the van!'

'Over there?'

'No! Over there!'

Dachshund Spotting Total:
Anthony 8, Holly 1, David 1

It's always this way—everything is dropped, those asleep are now awake, and Fruit Ninja is abandoned mid-swipe. No one wants to miss seeing the dachshund.

As I watch the cute sausage dog, I'm smiling with the rest of them, but I'm beginning to wonder if I'll see one on this trip. I have a sinking feeling I'm going to get to the end without having spotted one. For some stupid reason, it brings tears to my eyes. I'm missing Charlie and Coco so much and don't want to think about returning home. Coco's death will seem more real then. Now it seems like a bad dream, as if when we return home, she will still be there with Charlie. When I'm reminded she's gone, it hits hard every time.

If not for Anthony though, we would have had eight less dachshund sightings. As much as we all curse him under our breaths for catching sight of the sausage dogs, the reality is *we* probably wouldn't have seen them. But man, surely it's my turn now—I was actually looking this time after David's call! The title is slipping farther and farther from my grasp.

Ye Olde Gem of a Towne

According to my vast research, in smaller cities, it is highly recommended to stay in the 'old town,' as outside of it, it is usually like any other modern town with normal buildings and no historical punch. And as we pull into Tallinn, one of the best-preserved medieval cities in Europe, I'm happy I took the time to research this little gem. Wow.

After checking into our hotel, the Savoy Boutique Hotel, that offers a free drink at the bar for each guest (soft drink for the kids, of course), we dump bags in what are quite beautiful hotel rooms, rug up in our winter gear, and set out for a walk to check out the gloriously medieval Tallinn.

We walk along narrow cobblestone streets lined with restaurants, beer halls, bars, and shops nestled inside gorgeous old buildings dating back to the fifteenth and sixteenth centuries. One of the oldest merchant houses dates back to 1410, and the town hall is even older, dating to the late 1300s. I feel like we've entered a 'Ye Olde Times Medieval Village,' and I can understand why it's a major tourist attraction for Estonia. There are old-fashioned stalls, wooden wagons with arching white canopies selling roasted nuts and mulled wine, manned by people looking like they stepped out of the fifteenth century. Even staff out the front of restaurants are dressed up, calling out in ye-olde speech to lure people in to eat.

As we pose for photos in the early evening at Viru Gate, the entrance to the old town with its ancient city walls and towering terracotta-tipped defense towers, I'm excited and a bit giddy. The atmosphere here is like nothing in Australia. I love it. Anthony gives me the 'I told you so' look and a little smile, reminding me I didn't want to go to the Baltics originally. In fact most people that we told we were going to Estonia, Latvia, and Lithuania, asked, 'But why would you go there?' Our response, 'Why not?'

Initially I had this elaborate itinerary of river cruises and trips into vampire territory to Transylvania, but it was too far out of the way for this trip. Egypt was on the agenda as well until dangerous riots made it a tricky destination to travel to. Other itineraries were designed and discarded many times over. When Anthony suggested the Baltics, I was hesitant, but only because I didn't know anything about Estonia, Latvia, and Lithuania. But isn't that what travel is all about? Not to say I don't want to go to Romania or Egypt at a later date—but right now, as I stand in this lovely little town, I feel so deeply a part of history that I'm happy we came.

History Lessons with Christina

We meet Christina after breakfast for a walking tour of the old town. At four degrees Celsius, it is a cold day. As usual I'm keeping a close watch on the weather websites for snow. I've checked them all, hoping that one will tell me what I want to hear. My favourite website shifts back and forth between Wunderground and Weather.com, depending on its prediction for snow or not. Where are you, snow? Why do you not eddy around me in magical swirls?

Tallinn has such an interesting history. It's been independent since 1991 after gaining freedom from Soviet occupation. Before that, going all the way back to 1154, it's been ruled by either the Swedes, Danes, or Poles, and was occupied by Nazi Germany until the end of World War Two.

According to Christina, Estonia has an uneasy relationship with Russia. They have not yet forgotten their bleak existence behind the Iron Curtain for so many years when thousands of people were killed, deported, and arrested.

We wander behind Christina learning about the history of Tallinn, with the kids photo bombing nearly every photo I take. I have hundreds of photos with the kids' crazy-eyed, goofy, grinning faces blocking the main feature of what would be a great photo. If only they'd let me put a few up on my private travel blog. But no, they are happy to photo bomb, but not so happy for me to post any of the photos for family and friends at home.

Old Tallinn has an upper town, Toompea, and a lower town. In olden times, the nobles lived at the top, and the merchants and bondsman lived below. A gate was closed at night to separate the two. Christina led us up a street called the Short Leg to the upper town to show us the parliament building and the Alexander Nevsky

Cathedral before strolling through the winding streets to a portion of the old city walls with a café at the top. Christina says it is a bit of an awkward climb up a ladder to get to the café, so Maree, David, and Mum decide to give the cafe a miss. But luckily, at the bottom, nestled into an alcove in the wall, is a timber cart selling mulled wine. Don't mind if I do!

Christina tells us the reason Tallinn still has such well-preserved fourteenth and fifteenth century buildings is because of hundreds of years of poor economics. The country simply couldn't afford to pull down its old buildings and rebuild. Nowadays, this is fabulous for tourism. A UNESCO World Heritage site since 1997, Tallinn is becoming more and more popular every year, and the crowds in summer, as Christina puts it, are 'not so funny anymore.' Again, I'm glad we are travelling in off-peak and don't mind the cold of early winter.

Farther along from the old town is the busy port and harbour. Tallinn is one of the busiest passenger ports in the Baltic Sea, and Christina points out the large ferry in the distance that zips back and forth to Finland. Some people work in Helsinki and catch the forty-five-minute ferry back and forth every day.

Gazing outwards, following Christina's pointed finger towards Finland, I wish for a bit more time on the holiday. Everything is so close together in Europe, but we had to pick and choose between the places to visit and the places to miss. I can't believe all the amazing countries we are passing by and don't have time to see.

There isn't much left of the day, but we decide to go on the rickety, older than usual, hop-on, hop-off sightseeing bus without getting off. The modern town is a little rundown here and there, and not particularly pretty from what I can see from the bus.

We are taken past the port, a jail, and the walls of an ancient monastery, monuments, churches, and old buildings. I enjoy the trip, but if I knew Anthony would see two more dachshunds from the bus, two brown, longhaired miniatures, I would have suggested another activity, like blindfolding Anthony.

Dachshund Spotting Total:
Anthony 10, Holly 1, David 1

Reflecting on Anthony

I want to see a dachshund so badly, but I do not have the eyes of an eagle or Anthony's laser-sharp focus. I'm often in a world of my own; even when I look like I'm concentrating, more than likely I'm not. Anthony usually has peace and quiet to watch the world go by and must be coaxed into long conversations, another reason why I often wish my dad were there. He was a talker and could not be ignored.

Don't get me wrong, my dad, Ross, did like the sound of his own voice—his companion in a chat need not respond much. A nod or a comment here and there would suffice, but Dad was an engaging man who livened conversations and had he been there, I think Anthony would have talked more. Anthony is much like David, his dad, but quieter again. Quite the conversationalists when you get them started, but also happy to sit and ponder.

To me, Anthony is not fully relaxed still. Three years ago when he, the kids, and I went on a jaunt around Western Europe and the UK, he was between roles at work, so it was the most relaxed I'd seen him in years. But on this trip, he's still working some of the time. When arriving at hotels and hooking up to the Internet to check Facebook and contact home (or me logging into my travel blog), Anthony is generally on the laptop responding to work emails.

I move to sit with Anthony and hold his hand. He smiles and reminds me that he has seen ten dachshunds. 'Ten,' he repeats.

'I'll catch up,' I reply feebly, to which he slowly shakes his head. Ha! I know he is right.

There are fleeting moments on the trip when I wish it were just us, not often though. As I said, they are fleeting and I couldn't ask for a more loving Mum or parents-in-law.

We all get along really well, but I have more people to pay attention to and organise. I love all of these people so much, and we're on the trip of a lifetime, but every now and then I feel a little caught in the middle trying to pay attention to the kids *and* focus on what the grandparents are saying while at the same time trying to carve out some time for Anthony and me. After a few weeks on the road, it is a little harder than I thought, but I wouldn't have it any other way. I'm so thankful for my family.

A Night Out

Being an over-planner, months ago I'd booked us into a restaurant called Peppersacks for dinner, a medieval restaurant serving up traditional Estonian food. The restaurant is busy, with tables filled with chatting, laughing people under the high, dark-timbered ceiling and shining chandeliers. We're led upstairs by staff wearing medieval attire and into a small, shadowed alcove dining area. We dine on pumpkin and parsnip soup, beef soup, garlic bread, Kessler chop, sauerkraut, lamb chops, chicken, and pork. We all tasted one another's dishes, sipped on Estonian beer, and then came the dessert. Lucky we're doing so much walking!

After dinner a belly dancer begins to shimmy away near our table to the cheers of the other patrons. As we leave there is a fierce sword fight performance between two feuding lords on the stairs. There are punches thrown, crossed swords, and a masked, sabre-wielding fiend who looks like he is about to end them both, but all he came in for was a beer. As he left, he passed it to David on his way out. What a great night!

It is after we leave the restaurant in the rainy night that I get lost. As we all dash out, I pause briefly to take a photo and, *voila*, just like that, everyone else is gone. It's raining quite heavily, and we don't have umbrellas, so I understand the rush. But it's dark, and I have no idea which way is up. A few minutes pass in which I am disorientated, but luckily I peer down a street, and there is David waiting on the corner in the rain, the only person in the eerie darkness. I am so thankful I could cry. Dads are awesome. And my photo was blurry, not worth the frustration of being lost. From now on, I might consider when it is a good time for a photo. I will also carry my own map.

I'm sorry to leave Tallinn so soon. There are so many little streets and shops, artisans and markets, and I would have loved another day to look around. But it's time to move on—to Latvia!

RIGA, LATVIA

Date: *November 10*
Location: *Tallinn – Riga*
Nights: *3*
Dachshunds so far: *12*

Pizza Rations

When we arrive in Riga, the driver eases carefully through the narrow streets until he comes to a one-way lane and parks in front of a beautiful art nouveau building, which houses our apartment hotel, Neiburgs. I'm looking forward to our three nights in Riga as Anthony, the kids, and I are in a big, two-level apartment. Woo-hoo!

Riga's old town is beautiful, with narrow cobblestone streets, lamp lights beginning to flick on, and market stalls and wagons with roasted nuts for sale. Even though Riga is larger than Tallinn, we reach the edge of the old town quite quickly.

Near to dinnertime a restaurant called Charlie's Pizza draws Sam in. It's like he has a pizza radar. We're missing our boy Charlie and we love Italian, so it's a quick decision.

'What are we having for dinner?', 'When are we having dinner?' and, 'Can we have pizza?' are Sam's most commonly asked questions as evening approaches, or even as early as the last bite of his lunch goes down his gob. Plus, it's been three days since his last pizza, people. Three days! How is a teenage boy meant to survive on such awful rations? Sam is as much on the lookout for Italian restaurants as he is for dachshunds.

I have to admit I would have preferred more of a local flavour, but it's the kids' holiday too, and we have three days here to sample the cuisine. And who doesn't love pizza made by Charlie? The answer—no one.

Their Prejudice. My Pride

The next day we prepare to meet Valdis, our guide for our walking tour of Riga. Initially I ignore the kids' imploring look and question, 'Do we have to go?'

Walking tours are proving not to be their favourite thing. Unless there is some kind of animal (squirrel, pigeon, cat, or even rat) or some type of sweet treat along the way, then the walking tour gets a bit of a thumbs down. But I'm hoping details we hear on the tours will sink into their brains. Sam spends more of his time jumping over cracks in the pavement and leaping up onto walls and steps than listening to the tour guide, and Holly loves practicing her new favourite activity of attempting to catch a pigeon.

I get that the history of Riga is not super interesting to kids, but they are skipping school, and Sam is happily missing out on studying *Pride and Prejudice* in English class—not a favourite read for teenage boys.

But what kid wouldn't be excited if their parents announced, 'Right kids, we're taking you out of school for weeks to travel the world!'

And the kids *were* excited, don't get me wrong, and in hindsight, perhaps Russia and the Baltic States weren't the best choice of travel destination with children. However, right now as they ask, 'Do we have to go?' I answer with something along the lines of 'Do you realise how lucky you are? Look interested, kids, or there's no hot chocolate afterwards!'

History Lessons with Valdis

It's getting colder, and at only one degrees Celsius outside and a bit drizzly, Valdis tells us the basic history of Riga inside the hotel foyer, going back to ancient times and the first known settlers of the site—the Livonians (Vikings).

We stroll through the main square of the old town, past the House of Blackheads, a merchants' guild house dating back to the fourteenth century, Saint Peter's Church, Saint Savior's Church, and stunning art nouveau buildings, for which Riga is famous. Valdis explains there are over eight hundred art nouveau buildings constructed in Riga during an economic boom in the late nineteenth and early twentieth centuries. I snap photo after photo of elaborate facades decorated with lions, sphinxes, statues, stained glass, flowers, sculptures, and gargoyles.

We are then led inside a building and down a set of stairs to see the thirteenth century foundations of the city. For some reason, the walls of the stairwell are decorated with Rotary International pennants from clubs all around the world. Rotarians David and

Maree study them. If only they had one from their hometown to add to the collection!

On the border of the old town and new, in a pretty riverside park, the beady eyes of all scan the grassy knolls and pathways for wandering dachshunds. None are seen, so the focus returns to Valdis as he points out the soaring forty-two-metre high Riga Freedom Monument, erected in 1935 to commemorate soldiers killed in the Latvian War of Independence. It is a monument to fallen soldiers, but also the site of official ceremonies in Riga. Valdis explains that today, the eleventh of November, is an important day for Latvians—Lacplesis Day, the day Latvians commemorate the Russians being driven from Riga by Latvian freedom fighters during the Latvian War.

We also learn that Latvia dealt with many incomprehensible atrocities during its occupation by Nazi Germany—the worst being the Rumbula massacre. Twenty-five thousand Latvian Jews were killed over a two-day period in late 1941 in Rumbula Forest near Riga. In short, they were marched to the site, ordered to disrobe, and then sent into pits, single file, and ten at a time. They were then ordered to lay face down upon the dead and dying at their feet. Then they were shot. It is so difficult to understand how things like this could—and can still—happen.

Eleven, Eleven

The eleventh of November is Australia's Remembrance Day, as well as many other countries around the world. It is a day to honour all those who died and suffered in war but also the commemoration for the date the hostilities in World War One officially ended at the eleventh hour of the eleventh day of the eleventh month in 1918.

Normally at home I'd be watching the ceremonies on television and trying not to cry when observing the minute's silence at 11:00 am. The mournful sounds of the 'Last Post' gets me every time.

After crossing a gently arching bridge decorated with hundreds, if not thousands, of padlocks of lovers, we stroll through the dachshund-less park and reenter the old town of Riga to visit the Musicians of Bremen Monument next to Saint Peter's Church.

The monument, gifted to Riga from the town of Bremen in Germany, is a bronze sculpture with a donkey, dog, cat, and rooster standing on each other's backs. Based on a Brothers Grimm fairytale *The Town Musicians of Bremen*, the monument to Valdis represents unity and strength: 'Alone we are weak, but together we are strong.' To be brief, in the fairytale, the four animals stand on each other's backs to take on robbers, and together they scare them away. The monument is about unity and strength, but also a political statement as the animals 'peer through the Iron Curtain' to a view of independence from Russia. Erected in 1990, Latvia, along with so many other countries, gained its independence from the Soviets one year later.

The noses and toes of the animals on the monument are golden, their dark bronze colour rubbed off by the hands of thousands of people who touch them for good luck. We all touch as well, seeing how far we can reach. All the ladies can only reach as far as the dog, but David, Anthony, and Sam reach to the cat. Only the tall people of the world, or those with stepladders, will reach the rooster, but its crest is as shiny as the rest of the animals.

It is at this point David decides to reveal his new accessory to keep the bitterly cold air at bay. He pulls a black balaclava over his face, with round holes for his mouth, eyes, and nose. Looking like he is about to murder someone, he grins happily from behind his mask as we all laugh.

The Baltic Way

As we walk back to the hotel, Valdis tells us of the Baltic Way, a protest in 1989 on the fiftieth anniversary of the Molotov-Ribbentrop Pact, a non-aggression agreement between Germany and the Soviet Union along with a secret pact to divide Eastern Europe between them. Amongst other things, it was a ten-year agreement to not attack each other or support the enemies of each other, which Hitler broke with the invasion of the Soviet Union in 1941. The Baltic Way was a protest involving over one million people holding hands in a human chain for six hundred kilometres through the three Baltic countries from Tallinn to Riga to Vilnius to protest the Soviet occupation.

I am in awe of the courage and determination of the people of these countries to gain their independence. I can hear the national pride in the voice of Valdis as he talks of Latvia's liberation. In 1989, while I was in the height of my nightclub days, perm, and bad '80s fashion, all I had to be concerned about was when the DJ was going to play my favourite song or if my teased-up fringe was going to flop. And these people? They were fighting for their freedom and their lives. It's humbling, to say the least.

It is a miserably cold and rainy day, but it doesn't dampen our spirits, especially when we are dressed in the right gear, although I feel the chill, as my jacket isn't cut out for the weather. The only bare skin is our pale faces. After a while though, the warm apartment beckons, so we stay in for a few hours for card games, catching up on my travel blog, and endless clapping games of Concentration, which I am slowly mastering. It is fun to run through all the places we've visited so far on the trip whilst clapping like a crazy person. Fun that is, until you've done it ten times over. But lucky for Holly, she has Mum and Maree to beg to play with her.

After dinner, even though I was in full sloth mode, Anthony suggests a walk. I almost say no but change my mind, and somehow we convince the kids to join us. We wind our way along the pretty lamp-lit streets to the new city and back around again. On our return we see hundreds and hundreds of people streaming from darkened streets with candles in hand. We follow quietly along and watch as people, young and old, place lit candles within small glass jars on what looks like the ancient city walls of the old town, or perhaps it is Riga Castle, I am unsure. We assume it has something to do with Lacplesis Day and mingle with the quietly respectful crowds to have a closer look.

Uniformed teenagers hand out dark red and white ribbons and little Latvian flags to us with a smile, and we watch mesmerised over the next half-an-hour as hundreds more people stream from the city with their candles and flags. It is ethereal, and we don't want to leave, but decide to walk all the way back through the old town to the Freedom Monument to see if anything is happening there.

At the Freedom Monument there are more candles, people, and wreaths of flowers. A man stands on the top step, singing. It is so moving to stand amongst the hushed crowds in the darkness with hundreds of flickering candles brightening the base of the monument. I am so thankful to Anthony who always wants to go for walks, especially in the evening, as I would have hated to miss this.

Dachshund Time

Anthony returns from his chilly morning jog with reports of a dachshund spotting. He can have it, as you won't catch me jogging in the cold, but we want to know all about it, of course. Black or brown? Longhaired or smooth? The verdict: brown smooth haired with a blue coat.

Dachshund Spotting Total:
Anthony 11, Holly 1, David 1

This morning we have a Skype date with Charlie and our neighbour, Angela. Charlie is dressed up for the occasion with a polka dot bowtie. He is adorable! He has absolutely no idea what is going on, is constantly jumping on Ange and trying to lick her face, but we don't care! It's so wonderful to see him (and Ange too). I try to claim it as a dachshund sighting, but Anthony promptly denies it.

Charlie is being so well cared for between our lovely neighbours and our house sitters, who are all dear friends. He couldn't be more spoilt, and it makes us all feel better to see him. Holly is happy *and* sad. Happy to see Charlie but misses him so much that she often wants to go home.

Today is a free day and after breakfast we decide to visit the Museum of the Occupation of Latvia. On our way we pass thousands of candles on the city walls, the grass, footpaths, and on the steps of the Latvian Freedom Monument, with some still burning. There are hundreds more there now than last night.

Anthony spots a black dachshund across the road from the Freedom Monument, and we manage to get a photo this time! They are elusive animals to capture on film.

Dachshund Spotting Total:
Anthony 12, Holly 1, David 1, the rest of us ZERO

'Dad,' asks Holly as they cross the road, 'how come you keep seeing all the dachshunds? It's not fair.'

Anthony grins, responding, 'That's because you're not looking. See these things here,' pointing to his eyes, 'they're for looking.'

'Tell you what,' he adds, after Holly insists with fervor that she is looking, 'I'll give you an advantage. Anyone who spots a leprechaun riding a dachshund can steal the dachshund-spotting title, regardless of points.'

'Well, that's never going to happen, Dad,' replies Sam.

'You never know,' Anthony offers, going back to his dachshund spotting.

'You don't know,' Holly adds with an air of certainty.

What made Anthony think of this, I do not know, but it starts a stream of fake leprechaun-riding-a-dachshund calls as we walk to the museum.

The Museum of the Occupation of Latvia is interesting, well—for the adults at least. In hindsight, perhaps finding a kid-friendly activity may have been better, but it's a short visit, and we learn more about the Soviet occupation, about which I had little to no knowledge. What is recorded at the museum is frightening and awful, even for the adults to think about, let alone the kids—

persecution, executions, and the deportation of thousands to Siberian prison camps where many perished.

Half a Pig

We finish our time in Riga at a traditional Latvian restaurant called Piejura. Decorated in a nautical theme with dark timbers, ships wheels, and sails, we are seated in a raised booth up the back. Our meal, which is enjoyed by all, is bean soup with pork, vegetables, and bacon in a bread bowl, pork shalicks, baked potatoes, lamb and beef sausage, potato and bacon sausages in a creamy sauce, and Maree has half a pig. Not really, but it is a huge roasted pork knuckle and the only thing on the plate, except for some cabbage. She needs a little help to finish it off, but thankfully we have a teenager with us!

Mum and I have one more stroll through Riga after dinner. Around the corner from our hotel are narrow streets lined with boutique shops. I buy souvenirs and a few little items I will put away for Christmas presents. I also buy two little bottles of Latvian liqueur for my friend of Latvian heritage. I will carry them for another nine weeks before arriving home to find out her heritage is, in fact, Estonian.

Riga is so beautiful, and like most places we visit, I wish for one more day here.

(10)

VILNIUS, LITHUANIA

Date: *November 13*
Location: *Riga – Vilnius*
Nights: *2*
Dachshunds: *14*

A Most Amazing Toilet Stop

We stop on the way to Lithuania and wander through the cold drizzle to see the Hill of Crosses, a field with thousands *and* thousands of crosses, rosary beads, crucifixes, and icons of the Virgin Mary, all crammed together in the middle of nowhere. And no, it's not a cemetery, it's a huge pile of crosses, junkyard style, but tidy-ish with timber pathways meandering through it.

People visit the hill to leave a cross and say a prayer. It has become a site of Christian pilgrimage, and although the origins are not certain, the location is thought to be where the uprising in the Polish-Russian War in 1830 to '31 occurred. But whatever the reason, this is certainly a sight to see if you happen to be on the road between Riga and Vilnius and need a toilet stop.

Christmas Market Confession

It's almost dark and still raining when we arrive in Vilnius to our lovely hotel. It's exciting to see a Christmas tree in the foyer too. Ah, it's begun! The Christmassy stuff! 'Take a deep breath, Lisa, there's still a couple of weeks to go until the Christmas markets.'

Our visit to Europe and the UK in 2009 was the beginning of my Christmas market obsession. No matter how big or small, if there is a Christmas market, a Christmas tree, or Christmas decorations, I *will* be excited. When driving through England for a month in late November 2009, every town we came upon had the most delightful little Christmas market with a large Christmas tree, caroling schoolchildren, local wares, food, mulled wine, and Christmas decorations. As we drove into Salisbury in southern England, I remember letting out such a zealous and sudden squeal of excitement, it almost caused Anthony to have a car accident. Thinking something was wrong, he turned to me all worried, only for me to utter, a little under my breath, 'There's a Christmas market.'

We prepare to go out for a wander. Even though we are dressed in weatherproof gear, we gratefully accept the offer of umbrellas from the friendly hotel staff and step out into the early evening, passing by the glowing and decorative street lamps. The lights are an old-fashioned item that modern towns do not have. The beautiful lampposts line each street, some attached to buildings with curved filigree arms holding them aloft.

It's a little foggy and eerie as we walk farther through the town and past many 'beautiful old buildings' and down 'cobblestone' streets. I will sound like a broken record before this trip is finished, but it is what these old towns have—beautiful old buildings and cobblestone streets. I'm not making it up, but I could be more inventive with my descriptions. We've still got Krakow, Cesky Krumlov, Prague, Strasbourg, and Nuremberg to describe! Time to be a little cleverer with my words! Next time the word 'cobblestone' may be replaced with 'flagstone,' or 'streets with uneven stones that trip up Maree, David, and Mum.'

We have dinner at a Lithuanian restaurant with great food, filling up on pickles and pork, chicken, sausages, sauerkraut, beetroot, and 'Grandma's rissoles,' which Grandma had to order because she is a grandma. Again Mum and I comment on how Dad would have loved this food. We miss his company, of course. We miss his laugh and his seemingly endless knowledge about everything, but it is the food that prompts many of our talks about him.

History Lessons with 'Boris'

Our first tour today is with a man whom Anthony has named Boris, as none of us could remember his name. First we visit Saint Theresa's Church and walk under the Gate of Dawn, once the sixteenth century city gates but now a small chapel arching over the road with an icon of the Virgin Mary inside.

Boris then takes us to so many churches I think we must be on a church tour, including the gloriously Gothic Church of Saint Anne's, the Church of Saint Nicholas, the oldest church in Lithuania, the Orthodox Church of the Holy Spirit, the neo-classical Vilnius Cathedral with soaring columns, sculptures, and frieze. The Vilnius Cathedral is the main Roman Catholic Church of Lithuania and was thought to be, prior to Lithuania's conversion to Christianity, a site of pagan worship to the Baltic god, Perkanus, the god of thunder and storm and celestial elements.

The last church of the day is the Church of Saints Peter and Paul, a former monastery built in the seventeenth century, which is a brief drive out of town. The church is interesting, really it is, it is highly decorative inside with over two thousand stucco figures, but the time comes on all holidays in Europe when you hit the 'church wall,' so to speak, and I hit it today. This church proved to be worth the visit as Anthony spots a brown dachshund scampering through a park outside the church, bringing his total to thirteen.

Dachshund Spotting Total:
Anthony 13, Holly 1, David 1

Afterwards, back in the old town, we wander along the streets of the old Jewish Quarter, noticing the parliament buildings and Vilnius University. Boris fills us in on the history of Vilnius and its ancient beginnings in 1323 and Lithuania's horrific World War Two history. When Vilnius was captured by Nazi Germany in June 1941, they promptly set up ghettos for the Jewish community. Once called the 'Jerusalem of Lithuania,' Vilnius had a population of around a hundred thousand Jews. Only twenty-four thousand survived the mass murders that took place there during the Nazi occupation. Usually the Jewish people were simply herded into pits and shot, including ten thousand in one day in the Ponary Massacre. It is awful to comprehend.

We all chat about this as we walk. Although all the adults in the group knew varying degrees of World War Two history, none knew of this massacre or even the 'liquidation,' as Nazi Germany often referred to it, of thousands of Jews in Lithuania. Unless you are a war buff, there are so many things we never learn about. In

Australia, usually we're taught of what the Allies were involved in during the war, but not so much about what was going on in Eastern Europe. I feel privileged to be able to visit these countries and learn a little more about their history.

We head back to the hotel and go our separate ways to grab lunch. Not long after, we hear some exciting news: Mum has entered the competition with her first dachshund sighting! When in a cafe buying her lunch, a black one sat on her foot, and it looked like Charlie! Best dachshund spotting of the trip so far. Mum figures a dachshund sitting on her foot is the only way she is going to see one. An easy spotting!

Dachshund Spotting Total:
Anthony 13, Holly 1, David 1, Mum 1

After our lunch break, we are driven out into the Lithuanian countryside by Boris to visit Trakai Castle, an island castle surrounded by the calm waters of Lake Galve. Built in the fourteenth century for the Grand Duchy of Lithuania, it fell into disrepair at the beginning of the seventeenth century and has only been restored in the last fifty years.

Boris fills us in about the Grand Duchy and the extensive renovations that brought the castle back to its former glory. In the castle, there are armour, swords, artwork, coins, old relics, and mounted heads of deer that Sam is not allowed to touch even though he tries. We walk in the ancient and dry moat, lock the kids up in the stocks in the castle grounds, and manage to avoid the souvenir shop as it is closed for the season. This is a huge disappointment for the kids . . . but thankfully Holly sees a swan, and Sam kicks some rocks and autumn leaves around, and is the fastest up the stairs, faster than anybody else, so not such a bad end to the day.

For dinner all are in agreement about heading back to our all-time favourite Lithuanian restaurant to order more meat, pickles and potatoes, sauerkraut, beetroot, schnitzel and another serving of Grandma's rissoles. It's a great night in the dimly lit cellar of the restaurant.

After dinner Anthony, Sam, Holly, and I step back out into the cold for a big walk around the old town. Vilnius is a nice mix of old and newer architecture with only a few medieval buildings, lovely eighteenth and nineteenth century buildings, church steeples dotting the skyline, and some interesting-looking shops I wouldn't have minded looking through had we more time. But it's time to move on and an early night as we have a 4:30 am pick-up for our flight to Poland.

(11)

KRAKOW, POLAND

Date: *November 15*
Location: *Vilnius – Warsaw – Krakow*
Nights: *5*
Dachshunds so far: *16*

Denied, My Friend!

Our final destination is Krakow, but our flight is to Warsaw. Why? The flights from Vilnius to Krakow were hideously expensive and involve connections like *Vilnius>Vienna>Krakow* (check a map—this is like flying way past Krakow and coming back again!).

Driving? Being transported through Belarus, a country I'd never heard of before considering driving through it, was a no-go due to visa complications. After working out that flying from Vilnius to Warsaw and hiring a driver to take us from Warsaw to Krakow was very economical compared to the other options, I booked it.

After a quick flight, we land in Warsaw, and our wonderful transport company awaits us for our road trip. The closer to Krakow we come, or every time we pass through a town, the dachshund scanning starts. Anthony sits up a little straighter in his seat, and with an owl-like turning of the head, he views parks, pathways, and streets (a slight exaggeration, but just go with it. Ha!). Either way he is very observant, and while I'm losing another Fruit Ninja battle and the grandparents are reading or playing games on their iPads, that is when dachshunds emerge from their underground lairs to prance about the streets with their waggy tails and winter coats to catch Anthony's eye.

Whenever I do notice Anthony scanning the landscape with a little lift to his chin, I sit up straighter, as do the kids, Maree, David, and Mum. We look through the windows of the van, but there are no sausage dogs to be seen, not even one bearing a leprechaun on its long back. And then, with a shout, there's a possible sighting by Anthony just before we reach Krakow. There are too many obstacles in the way for a confirmation to be made though. Denied, my friend!

We arrive to our hotel, which is on the edge of the old town of Krakow opposite a beautiful park, and as we're unloading suitcases, a horse and carriage clip-clops past with relaxed, smiling tourists within. Seconds later we four ladies decide it is something we need to do. Not want. *Need.*

As usual after settling in quickly, we head out for a wander down to the old town and Krakow's main square. Anthony refers to the map and off we go, with Maree staying close behind him. She says it's because she doesn't want to get lost, but I suspect she has an ulterior motive of dachshund spotting as Anthony is cutting through the park to lead us to the centre of the old town. No long-bodied dogs appear, but we like watching Maree run to catch up to Anthony.

Open Letter to the Group, re: Anthony's Walking

It's not my fault Anthony walks at the speed of light. Maree and David made him. I blame them entirely. Don't look at me for help, people! Keep up or we are all doomed to be lost and wandering in circles. Although, truth be told, after becoming lost in Tallinn, I now carry my own map, but I'm also taking the photos, spreading my attention between six people, typing notes in my phone for the travel blog, and answering constant questions, some as important as:

Why are pigeons grey? Do I have to walk? Can we have pizza for dinner? Is that a dachshund? What time is dinner? Can we go in that tourist shop? What time is dinner again? When are we going to get there? What are we doing today? How many dachshunds has Dad seen? Do we have to go into another church? Can I buy that? Can I buy this? Can I have an ice cream? How about a hot chocolate? Why couldn't we bring Charlie with us? Can I call that pigeon Dave? Can you play Concentration with me?

#FirstWorldProblem

We arrive to Krakow's main square—wow! I love it. Dating back to the thirteenth century, it's the largest medieval square in Europe. Our first sight is of the expansive Cloth Hall, a long, covered market hall. Originally a market for cloth, it soon became a European centre for trade during the fifteenth century, selling salt from the salt mines, spices, and more.

Next to it is the towering Town Hall Tower, the only thing left standing after the demolition of the town hall. The Gothic tower is a massive seventy metres tall. As darkness falls and the lights begin to shine on the tower and the Cloth Hall, it is so pretty I take a photo.

The full length of the Cloth Hall is filled with neat and tidy stalls selling handmade wooden crafts, jewellery, and souvenirs. Maree has her eyes on some beautiful amber earrings, a gemstone for which Poland is famous. Anthony spots a tiny silver dachshund sitting on a bed of amber. It is swiftly bought, along with a Christmas tree decoration from Krakow for our tree in New York City. We exit the other end of the hall to find ourselves in front of the queue of horse and carriages, ready to cart tourists around the town.

It is a little early, but soon the Christmas markets will start, and what is already a beautiful square will light up even more with stalls, an ice-skating rink, and Christmas trees. I wish we could've been in Krakow for the Christmas markets, but no matter how much I'd fiddled with the itinerary I hadn't been able to make it work. I'm super disappointed, but you know, #FirstWorldProblem. I think I'll survive, just.

Remembrance

Mum is quiet. As we walk around Krakow Square, she remarks to me that Dad would have loved this. 'I wish he were here,' she comments, looking around the square.

Tears sting at my eyes. I wish he were here too. He died so suddenly from pneumonia after his lung cancer diagnosis that for a long time, it didn't seem real. After a rushed helicopter flight from a small country hospital to Sydney, Mum drove the five-hour journey, and we all met him at the other end. We did not just find a very ill man who was preparing for a cancer battle, but a man whose lungs were filled with fluid, his body and organs shut down, and the only thing keeping him alive was a ventilator pumping oxygen into his failing body. Dad was still alive, yet not.

Looking back, I know we had the opportunity to say good-bye, something many people don't get but wish desperately for. We had time to cuddle him, hold his hand, and be together. We had time to call family, time to have the children brought to the hospital from school by Maree and David. The kids had time to fill up their grandpa's cuddle box until it was full, so he always had their cuddles with him.

Holding Dad's hand while the ventilator was turned off was the most heart-breaking thing I've ever been through. The moment the life-giving oxygen stopped flowing around his body, he passed right in front of us, faded away more quickly than I thought was possible—and he was gone. And even though the doctors had told us that his lungs were ruined, it didn't stop me from holding my *own* breath, hoping he'd draw one after the ventilator was turned off. But he didn't. Every time I think about it, my throat closes over. I can't imagine how Mum feels.

His presence is missed at family events. He was the conversation starter and had a big sense of humour, which I miss every day. He whistled all the time, hummed when he held his grandchildren, and gave the best cuddles—cuddles that I know will never be replaced in my lifetime. His brother, my Uncle Phillip, is the only one that comes close.

I link arms with Mum as we circle the square looking for somewhere for dinner, and we talk of Dad. They were together for fifty years. It's a long time to have someone by your side, someone to walk with, to hold hands with, and share a laugh. A fifty-year bond is irreplaceable. He's been gone two years, but she still doesn't like walking into a room on her own or being the odd one out at a table of couples. The trip has stirred up her grief, and she misses him, more than ever, but to look at her you wouldn't realise it unless you note she is a little quiet.

I'm so sad for her. I want to see her ambling along with Dad and enjoying this with him. She is included, and she is loved, but I see Maree and David together, Anthony and I have each other, and it pains me for her to not have Dad by her side. When I start to think about family, I want my sister here with us as well, and I'm looking forward to seeing her in New York City.

Mum and I are distracted from these thoughts by the beauty of Krakow's square. Isn't it what we all want—distraction? These are things we cannot change. We learn to adapt but never forget.

Dinner is early tonight, and we laugh and chat, but all are tired after our 4:30 am start. We stroll along the narrow cobblestone streets of the old town back to our hotel, kiss and hug Maree, David, and Mum, and head to our rooms.

We settle into our hotel room together, just Anthony, the kids, and me, cuddling and chatting until it's time for bed. Holly snuggles into bed with Anthony and me for a bit, talking about Charlie and Coco. She is homesick again and misses Charlie desperately. She's enjoying the trip but at the same time wants to go home to see him. But like me, she is also dreading our return, as Coco won't be there to greet us.

Krakow Walking Tour with Barbara

It's walking tour time again, and the kids are so excited. Ha! I'm so funny.

Our first stop with our guide Barbara is Wawel Castle, a short walk from our hotel. It is set high up on Wawel Hill where there is evidence of settlement all the way back to the Stone Age. Built by Casimir III the Great, the fourteenth century castle has housed the monarchy of Poland for hundreds of years. Looming high above the Vistula River, it's an obvious vantage point for a castle and quite a steep walk up to reach it. After a call from Mum, Sam crooks his arm to give her some extra support, before Maree joins her on the other side.

Firstly we enter the nine hundred-year-old Wawel Cathedral, the Basilica of Saints Stanislaus and Wenceslas. Kings have been crowned and buried here, including King Casimir III the Great in a carved red limestone sarcophagus. The cathedral is beautiful inside, but you'll have to take my word for it, as we aren't allowed to take photos.

Down below on the parklands surrounding the castle is a metal sculpture of a fire-breathing dragon. Again, you will have to take my word for the 'fire-breathing' bit, as I'm not quick enough with the camera, no matter how long we wait there. The dragon rears up on what looks like an extra sets of legs, but upon a closer look, I realise they are heads. Seven heads. Strange! Every few minutes the main head of the dragon breathes fire, and a small flame shoots from its mouth. Children crowd around the base, squealing each time. Known as the Smok Wawelski, the dragon features in Polish folklore stories.

Legend has it that hundreds of years ago the dragon, which lived in a cave under Wawel Hill, terrified the people of Krakow. They offered him sacrifices of sheep every day, and a young maiden every year until there were no more maidens left except the King's daughter, Wanda. Brave knights tried to defeat the dragon but couldn't, until a cobbler's apprentice filled a sheep skin with brimstone and pitch, and made it look like a real sheep. When the dragon ate his daily offering, it burned in his tummy. He drank all the waters of the river until it was drained, but nothing worked. The dragon exploded, and the people of Krakow rejoiced. The King's daughter married the cobbler's apprentice, and all lived, as they say, happily ever after.

Afterwards Barbara led us through the Jewish Quarter, known as Kazimierz, and pointed out synagogues, Jewish schools, the Jewish market, and a monument to the tens of thousands of Krakow Jews who lost their lives in World War Two. It is quiet as we wind down narrow streets past cafes, art galleries, and an outdoor market. Shown to the world through the movie *Schindler's List*, Barbara takes us past a few areas featured in the film.

As we walk back towards the old town, a call rings out as Anthony sees a dachshund. I follow his pointed finger, and sure enough ahead in the distance is a darling brown miniature dachshund puppy. It's so cute!

Dachshund Spotting Total:
Anthony 14, Holly 1, David 1, Mum 1

Eventually we reach the old town square and cross to the fourteenth century Saint Mary's Basilica. The day is bright, and the square is filled with people and pigeons. Gathered in groups around restaurants and garbage bins, it's a child's delight. Sam spies the pigeons and yells out a fake dachshund call. Before we can say no, Sam races through a bunch, stirring up the pigeon party. Anthony gives an exasperated yell, but I can't help but smile a little. It's such a boy thing to do.

As we wait in the queue to enter the basilica, Barbara points out the highest tower of the church and tells us of the 'hejnal,' a traditional bugle call played from the tower. She says originally the call was played at the opening and closing of the city gates each day but is never played in full. It is cut short before the end, as long ago, when the bugler sounded the alarm of a Mongol attack, he was shot in the neck and didn't finish the bugle call. To honour him, the music is now played every hour on the hour, but is cut short each time.

We are distracted from Barbara by a bellow of a call from David, 'DACHSHUND!'

We follow his gaze, and there are two boisterous black dachshunds sniffing around the concrete bollards surrounding the church. And lucky for us, we all get to pat them. I can't believe we've seen THREE this morning.

Dachshund Spotting Total:
Anthony 14, David 3, Holly 1, Mum 1

Noticing our excitement about the dachshunds, Barbara tells us about the annual Krakow Dachshund Parade. Gesturing to the square, she says that almost two thousand paraded through last year, led in by a marching band. There is a competition for the best-dressed dachshund and best poster and slogan to convince people to buy dachshunds. Holly grabs Anthony's arm and begs him to let us bring Charlie next year to go in the parade. It will be the first thing we look for online as soon as we get back to the hotel.

Back to Saint Mary's Basilica—the church draws people not only for its beautiful interior of stained glass windows, frescoes, and gold trim, but the main attraction of the carved wooden altarpiece. Decorative panels open at midday every day to the sound of organ music to reveal the thirteen- by eleven-metre "Altarpiece of Veit Stoss," a Gothic altarpiece created in the fifteenth century. With two hundred painted and gold sculptures, I have to say it's absolutely stunning. I even have photographic evidence this time. There is a five zloty charge per camera ($1.70 AUD) to take photos in the church. It seriously strained the budget, but it was worth it.

It's the end of the tour, and I'm disappointed it didn't include a tour of the old town, so Anthony and I discuss going for a stroll around the old city walls later on. It is quite a cold day, so after a quick lunch of Polish borscht soup and pizza, we head back to the hotel for a relaxing afternoon. I'm glad for this little reprieve as I'm a little tired and way behind on the travel blog. The grandparents like their downtime too, the kids will never say no to lazing around, and Anthony has work to do.

Anthony still isn't as relaxed as I'd like. As I've said, on our last trip he was between roles, but this time he has some work things to attend to. However, I suspect it's more than that. This trip was his idea, wanting to recreate our wonderful trip in 2009. But I know it isn't playing out quite the same for him. The kids were younger then, happy to follow us wherever we led them, and I know some parts of this trip are not particularly interesting for them. We're both beginning to realise that the trip should have been planned with more collaboration with the kids. As much as all of these historical things are of interest to us, it's not always so interesting for them. And in hindsight, perhaps we should have had part of the trip with just the four of us, whether at the beginning or the end, or even for a week or two in the middle. While we are having an absolutely wonderful time with our parents, there is nothing like one-on-one family time with your own family unit too.

Anthony and I discuss the idea of a trip with each of the children when they finish high school, a last family trip with each of them before they start their adult lives—a trip where they choose the destination and the activities. We like the idea but decide not to tell them yet.

A Royal Procession

'Mum!'

I hear a call from the adjoining room, and Holly and Sam race in to me. They remind me we haven't yet looked at the dachshund parade! What? How have we been back at the hotel for a couple of hours and not looked on YouTube? Where are our priorities?

OMG! It is hilarious. We are rolling on the bed, crying with laughter, and watching it over and over again. Before long we run like loonies to Mum's room and then to Maree and David's hotel room to make them watch.

Not only do we learn the Polish word for wiener, sausage dog, or dachshund is jamnik, but also there is a crowned king and queen of the parade. They are dressed up in all sorts of different costumes, and dogs come in from all over the world. Can you believe it?

The parade begins at noon after the hejnal bugle call from the tower of Saint Mary's Cathedral, and the jamniki begin their parade—called the Royal Route as it follows the same route as Polish royal coronations and processions. They really are as important as kings and queens, so it makes sense. Holly wants to bring Charlie now more than ever!

After fun and hilarity we head to a traditional Polish restaurant for dinner. Everyone enjoys the food, except me who made a bad choice of some tasteless chicken in a yucky sauce, but everyone else's meal of fried dumplings, golabki—meat and rice wrapped in cabbage leaves with a creamy tomato sauce—beef stew, potatoes, beetroot, and veggies are nice. And I know because I tasted them all!

After dinner Anthony, Sam, Holly, and I go for a big walk around the main square, the old town walls, and the base of Wawel Castle. On the way back Holly spots a wirehaired dachshund in a park. It is so cute! The wirehaired dachshund is a not-often-seen dachshund in Australia, and I don't think I've ever seen one until now. With wiry coats and scruffy eyebrows and beards similar to a Scottish terrier, they are adorable. Top-notch sighting, and I think it should get extra points, but Anthony denies it. One point only to Holly.

Dachshund Spotting Total:
Anthony 14, David 4, Holly 2, Mum 1

Five dachshunds in one day! Not bad, Krakow. Not bad. I'm going to be watching and hoping for a sighting of my own. We might have to come back for the dachshund parade one day.

Auschwitz – Birkenau

We arrive early to Auschwitz I. Fog clings to the two-story buildings, shrouding leafless winter trees and the barbed wire fencing. As we make our way to the Auschwitz-Birkenau Memorial and Museum, it's eerie and quiet except for the hushed tones of our guide and the gravel crunching under our feet.

The details we see and hear at the museum are hard to comprehend. It is difficult to look at the exhibits of thousands of pairs of shoes, glasses, combs, brushes, two tonnes of human hair originally gathered to make blankets and cloth, and suitcases with names, addresses, and dates of birth marked clearly on the outside. It is even more difficult to walk through the cramped underground chambers where people were tortured and past the execution wall where many were shot. It is even harder to walk through the room where there are photos of children with tiny dirty faces. They stand with their families after arriving at the camp, wide-eyed and innocent. Holly can't even look. None of us can. We are not allowed to talk in this room, signs ask for silence, so I can't comfort the children or talk to them about anything. We do not stay in there long.

We pass through the main gate of Auschwitz II-Birkenau, aptly named the 'Gate of Death,' and even as the day brightens the fog refuses to lift. It is mid-November and heading into winter, so it's no surprise. In such a sad place it seems fitting.

Stark ruins of rows upon rows of barracks stretch into the distance bordered by barbed wire and wooden watchtowers, and intersected by the railway line that brings tears to my eyes every time I look at it. At the end of the line is Crematorium I, the largest gas chamber at Auschwitz I, where up to seven hundred people were exterminated at once. They were told they were going in the chamber to be showered and for delousing. Instead they were locked inside and gassed with the chemical Zyklon B.

It is incredibly sad and unsettling to walk the same path along the railway line as those who were led to the gas chambers. It's a long walk, and all in the group are quiet. Maree and Mum are tight-lipped, as am I. I listen to the guide, but not everything registers with me. I know I will forget things about this day, but it doesn't seem right to be jotting notes on my phone, and I don't want to.

At the end of the line are the ruins of Crematorium I, which was burned down just before the camp was liberated. A black marble memorial stretches along where it once stood, and in what was a place of death and despair is now a shrine to remember those lost. It is dotted with candles and red and white roses.

We enter cold, barren bunkhouses that once housed five hundred or more prisoners. They are not airtight, are unlined, and are little more than stables. Cool air swirls through the room. It is a cold day, but not the freeze of full winter, and I cannot imagine how people survived even this, let alone starvation, hard labour, and disease.

I can't help but picture the images from the museum, the faces of children and the tired, hungry, and dirty people who, with their families, had been herded onto trains like cattle. And after days encased in these carriages, they arrived here, disembarking finally in fresh air only to be sent to the gas chambers.

I feel a little ill walking around, and Anthony and I discuss whether we should have brought the children here, especially Holly, who is only twelve. Anthony bundles Holly up and walks along with his arm around her shoulders. I'm incredibly proud of both of the children.

As adults we know of the inhumane cruelties in the world, but Sam and Holly are beginning to learn about this. Although Anthony and I don't want to burden them with too much, we feel it is important to learn about past mistakes in the world and to not forget about the victims of war.

It is with all the stories of war and death that I begin to think about the loss of Dad and Coco, and it all pales in comparison to the suffering in the world, past and present. My father was loved, lived a great life until sixty-five, and passed with his hands cradled in ours. Coco's life was cut short, at only two. I hate that she didn't live a full life, but the life she had was wonderful, and she was spoiled rotten.

There is a lot of horror and terror in this world, and we have lived lives free of those things. Grief, sadness, and heartbreak, yes. But horror and terror, no.

Something New

Later that day, after dinner back at the hotel, we hear from our house sitters and friends, Tracy, Aaron, and Marguerite. We watch videos of Charlie playing chase around our yard with their German shepherd, Merlot. That is, Merlot is loping around, tongue lolling, and Charlie is running at champion racehorse pace to even come close to catching her. He looks happy with company, and Anthony and I remark to each other that perhaps when we get home, he will need a new friend. We've never just had one dog. A new puppy, perhaps? Yes.

We tell the kids, and they're so happy Charlie will have a new friend to play with. They want to start searching on the Internet straightaway, but I want to wait till we get home. It's not time yet. But then Holly bursts into tears, worried we are forgetting about Coco. I assure her that Coco will *never* be forgotten. Just like we will never forget about *any* of our loved ones. 'They're always with us,' I whisper to her as we cuddle in bed.

Everyone else is fast asleep, but I can't settle. I try to jot down details of the day for the travel blog, but I don't want to. I am suddenly a bit teary. The atrocities we've heard about today won't clear from my mind, so instead I look online for a new puppy.

Snow Spotting

When Maree and David return from an early walk, they proudly display photographic evidence of a dachshund spotting in the park across from the hotel. It's Maree's first, and she's grinning from ear to ear. She even chased it down to get a photo! Maree running should get extra points for over and above effort, but it's denied. One point awarded only.

Dachshund Spotting Total:
Anthony 14, David 4, Holly 2, Mum 1, Maree 1

After breakfast we're picked up by our guide, Kate, for a nine-hour day trip to Zakopane, a village and ski resort at the foot of the Tatra Mountains near the border of Slovakia. Millions of people visit Zakopane, called 'Poland's winter capital,' every year for snow sports, mountaineering, and hiking. I want to see this village covered in snow, but I have my doubts!

Zakopane is a hundred kilometres away, and soon enough, once we leave the built-up areas, I can see little villages nestled amongst the hills with steeply gabled-roofed houses and woodpiles stacked up for winter.

The first stop in Zakopane is the Jaszczurowka Chapel, a timber church designed and built in 1904 by renowned architect Stanislaw Witkiewicz. The carvings inside are beautiful, as is the stained glass, but the most exciting part of the stop is . . . wait for it . . .

SNOW.

It's only a little bit of snow, or possibly frost that hasn't melted yet. But the experts in the discovery, Mum, Sam, and I, decide that it *is* snow. Kate then tells us that it's normally snowing by now and that soon it should be. According to Weather.com, there is a possibility of snow showers in the coming weeks. A possibility. My fingers are crossed.

But for now, Zakopane is almost balmy at ten degrees Celsius, and we see more blue sky than we've seen since we left Turkey.

We catch the funicular up to Mount Gubalowka to look over Zakopane. It's quiet up here now, but I can imagine it busy with skiers and snowboarders. The view over the lofty ridgeline of the snow-capped Tatra Mountains is spectacular. We linger, taking photos with the mountains as a stunning backdrop and counting the sheep wandering in the fields below where there is supposed to be snow. The chair lifts are halted, waiting for the season to begin.

Back in the village, we walk along the shopping area called Krupowki and past busy market stalls selling jewellery, souvenirs, and traditional folklore items. Many stalls are filled with pale yellow rolls that we are told is oscypec, a traditional Polish cheese. It is a smoked cheese made from sheep's milk, which, to be honest, looks like a bread roll. Kate says she doesn't think most of the cheese is still made with the old, traditional method, but mass produced for tourists.

After seeing Kate eating some of the warmed-up cheese lathered with raspberry jam, I decide to give it a try, and it's pretty good. Afterwards we have lunch at a Polish style My My (our favourite self-serve restaurant in Moscow) and feast on pork, potatoes, cabbage, Brussels sprouts, and more pork.

Dachshund Madness

As we are walking back to the tour van, Anthony yells a loud dachshund call. Not far ahead an older man is walking two big standard dachshunds, a tan and a black and tan, and they are gorgeous. We ask to have a pat, and the man says yes but then adds that the dogs always get the attention and pats, so Maree offers to pat him, which he gladly accepts with a laugh. The standards are so cute, with bigger paws, a deeper chest, and the cutest floppy ears!

Dachshund Spotting Total:
Anthony 16, David 4, Holly 2, Mum 1, Maree 1

An important event then occurred. I spotted my first dachshund out the window of the van! It was a close call between Anthony, Maree, and me. It is a relief, as I had a really bad feeling that spotting the most popular dog in the whole world (non-biased opinion) would elude me for the entire trip.

It is the day of dachshunds as only a minute later, Anthony spots another in a park, but it's so far away the rest of us with normal eyesight must wait to make sure. But as we drive closer, it is confirmed a genuine spotting. I do not know how he saw it; he must have dachshund radar. This brings his score to seventeen.

Dachshund Spotting Total:
Anthony 17, David 4, Holly 2, Mum 1, Maree 1, Lisa 1

A minute later Anthony spots another one! OMG! But this time it is *so* far away it cannot be confirmed, and even he is unsure. It is swiftly denied. No point for you, my friend!

Sam is on zero, but he's decided since it was his goal to see none, in his eyes he is winning. *If* he sees one, he is planning to auction off the sighting to the highest bidder.

The next morning, while I'm still lying in bed only dreaming of my next dachshund spotting, Anthony returns from a run with a report of seeing another one. It's getting crazy! I've never seen this many at home.

Dachshund Spotting Total:
Anthony 18, David 4, Holly 2, Mum 1, Maree 2, Lisa 1, Sam 0

Choose-Your-Own-Adventure Day

Our last day in Krakow is a free day, and we all have things we want to do. Maree and David are visiting the Wielezica Salt Mines. Mum is having a haircut, and Anthony, the kids, and I set out for a big walk around Krakow. And to ruin my snowy plans, the day is beautiful and sunny and so warm we don't need jackets. It's nice to have the sun on my face in spite of my wish for snow.

I finally manage to get an awesome photo of the Smok Wawelski, the dragon statue at the base of Wawel Castle breathing fire. I'm quite impressed with my photo.

I love the kids' interaction together on the holiday. On a holiday they only have each other, and as Anthony and I stroll along, they talk a lot, run, and play. It's lovely.

We see no dachshunds, but Sam, the only one who hasn't spotted one yet, has decided pigeon spotting is a better competition. He's seen a million at least, so he declares himself the winner. And after some pondering over the last few days, he also declares that all pigeons are officially called Dave. Holly continues her pigeon-catching efforts, and there is so much subsequent pigeon chatter from the children that eventually the topic is banned, at least temporarily.

We meet up with Mum for lunch and wander through the lovely streets surrounding the Krakow Market Square to shop. Sam buys a tiny glass dachshund, and Holly finds a t-shirt with a fire-breathing dragon on it (the symbol of Krakow). The reason Holly wants the shirt is because the dragon is walking a dachshund on a lead. I kid you not. They obviously like their dachshunds here. We need to come back in September and see this dachshund parade. It's on the bucket list.

After shopping we enter the main square, and I let out a pathetic fake sob at the sight before me. The sight is of chalets for the Christmas market in front of Saint Mary's Basilica *and* of a ginormous Christmas tree. We will miss the market by only a couple of days. I expect comfort after this sad event, and Holly gives it to me, as she is a good daughter.

'Mum, when is the first Christmas market?' she asks.

'Nuremberg,' I reply with a grin, 'It's one of the most famous ones in the world!'

Her eyes light up. 'I love Christmas!' she announces, as she stares up the huge tree in the square. 'I can't wait to see all the markets.'

'I can't wait to eat chocolate. Let's go.'

We walk past the empty market stalls to our destination, a chocolate shop and cafe we'd spotted a few days before. We see an interesting sticker on the door of the cafe featuring a brown dachshund with a line through it, like a no smoking sign.

We debate on its meaning. Is it: 'Don't share your chocolate with your dachshund' or 'No dachshunds allowed in the chocolate cafe'? We jokingly ponder whether all other breeds of dogs are permitted in the shop, or permitted chocolate, or is it only brown dachshunds that have to miss out? Can black dachshunds have chocolate or enter the shop? Ah, the dachshund talk is never-ending. We proceed to stuff our faces with chocolate-covered ice cream, hot chocolates, and chocolate cheesecake.

We then meet up with Maree, and us four ladies embark on our pre-planned carriage ride around the old town and Wawel Castle. It is a lovely ride, except I discover I am allergic to horses and spend most of the ride with red, itchy, watering eyes, a runny nose, and attempt to set a Guinness World Record for the most amount of sneezes in the time it takes to circle Krakow in a carriage. I snuggle up with Holly under the blanket and smile to my two mums, and in between sneezing, all I can think is how lucky I am.

After our lengthy five-night stay in Krakow, it's time to pack up, and I'm ready to go now. It was the perfect amount of time to explore the beautiful town of Krakow and an incredible, though difficult, opportunity to learn more about the Holocaust.

(12)

BUDAPEST, HUNGARY

Date: *November 20*
Location: *Krakow – Budapest*
Nights: *4*
Dachshunds so far: *27*

Travel Saviours

Months ago, organising today's drive through Slovakia to Budapest was when I started to do my own thing with bookings rather than use my local travel agent. Not only was the Vilnius to Krakow transport a slight issue, but Krakow to Budapest was as well. My agent was fantastic, honestly. She found us the most amazing flight deals, and was *so* helpful with many things. However, travel agents, I think, are sometimes limited in what their company has access to. For example, the only recommendation I was given to get from Krakow to Budapest without hiring our own car was to fly.

But there were no direct flights—except these: *Krakow>Berlin>Budapest*, which is like going backwards and then forwards again. Or this one: *Krakow>Vienna>Budapest* or even the ridiculous *Krakow>Berlin>Vienna>Budapest.* Not only were these options unnecessary, it was ridiculously expensive, not to mention the lengthy flight time.

I contacted a transport company in Poland and their return email says something along the lines of:

Yes, of course we can transport you to Budapest from Krakow by car, we do it all the time, and we can take you to a fabulous mountain restaurant in the hills for a scrumptious Slovakian lunch.

Scrumptious Slovakian Lunch

After a few hours driving through the beautiful countryside of Slovakia, we arrive at Koliba Pastiera Restaurant in Ruzomberok, for our scenic stopover. Nestled in the Cutkovska Valley and surrounded by the Tatra Mountains, the restaurant is built in the traditional Slovak architecture of wood, wood, and more wood, and has a warm and welcoming feel as we shuffle in out of the cold.

Seated in our own little, private dining room, we look through the menu. There are so many mouthwatering dishes to choose from, but finally we choose and enjoy a fantastic meal of pork schnitzel (cleverly disguised as 'breaded meat' on the menu), the most amazing goulash with chilies, baked potato, and sour cream served in a frying pan set on a wooden board, pork sausage, and gnocchi.

Deliberation on Pseudo-Sightings

As we leave the restaurant, there's a dachshund sighting, but it proves to be a genuine fake call. The fake dachshund calls have amped up lately, especially from Sam. Even pigeons are falling into the fake dachshund calls. It started simply if there was a vague four-legged creature far in the distance. A call is made just in case, only to find when we get closer, it's a terrier, a poodle, or even a bulldog. There are some ambiguous dogs that must have *some* dachshund in them, and there are often lengthy technical breeding discussions, like 'No, its ears aren't floppy enough,' 'Its legs are too long,' and 'Its nose/body isn't long enough.'

It *was* slightly hilarious, at first, when pigeons were called with the loud exclamation of 'Dachshund!' but after the tenth dachshund call, as we walk through a square filled with hundreds of pooping pigeons, it gets old *really* quickly. And then there are the cats, the fire-breathing dragon statues, and lizards that are also 'called.' Anthony, he of little patience, thinks we need to implement a deduction of dachshund points if there are too many fake calls, as does Holly. The competition is getting serious! Ha!

So, to explain this lengthy fake dachshund call discussion, the fake dachshund call by Sam as we leave the restaurant is a carved wooden statue of a Slovakian man. It is denied promptly with the threat of dachshund points deduction, but as Sam is on zero, he may have to start going into minus figures.

KFC to the Rescue

In the early evening, we arrive at the Marriott Executive Apartments in Budapest and enjoy spreading out in their spaciousness. The hotel is a little older, isn't so fancy, and is our first hotel with no free Wi-Fi. However, it has the best thing of all—a washing machine! Hallelujah! We shall be clean and no washing in a bathtub for a while. Yay!

For Wi-Fi our only option is to loiter near the KFC down the road from the hotel and use their free Wi-Fi. There isn't even any need to go inside. I can pick it up from about twenty-five metres away. Various people huddle up and down the street with devices clutched in hand, pilfering fried chicken-flavoured Wi-Fi in the cold.

We visit a local deli and supermarket for supplies and enjoy a night in, relaxing, washing clothes, and playing cards. While at the supermarket, I pick up some chocolate treats as Advent gifts for the kids. The first of December is not far away, and I need to stock up. An Advent calendar and chocolates are a yearly tradition for us (as with many people), but I try to make it interesting as most mornings the kids have to solve riddles, go on little treasure hunts, or sing Christmas carols to receive their gifts. Work for it, kids!

History Lessons with Motor-Mouthed Mary

We meet Mary, our guide for a city tour of Budapest. She is friendly and knowledgeable, but before too long, I realise it's not going to be my favourite tour of the holiday as she talks so fast and repeats herself so much that it's frustrating. Before long I feel the beginnings of a headache.

Firstly, we cross the Danube River from the Pest side to the Buda side to Castle Mount, home to Matthias Church and Fisherman's Bastion. Our first amazing view as we approach is of Fisherman's Bastion with the Spire of Matthias Church rising behind it.

Fisherman's Bastion looks like a castle and city walls, but it is a collection of terraces and towers along the banks of the Buda side of the Danube. It is thought that, in the Middle Ages, a guild of fisherman once protected this section of the city walls; hence it's called Fisherman's Bastion. The highly decorative bastion, with its seven towers, windows, arches, and arcades, was not built for defence, but to commemorate the thousand years of the Hungarian State.

Standing atop the bastion as we are now, we gaze to the Pest side of the river with its equally impressive buildings and bridges, including the mighty Gothic Revival structure of the Hungarian Parliament Building. We make our way down to the statue of King Stephen, the first king of Hungary, to watch a freewheeling hawk spiralling above before returning to its master, a falconer in medieval garb.

King Stephen founded Matthias Church, a once Gothic and now restored Baroque-style church, in 1015. I quite enjoy wandering through it, even though I have hit the 'church wall.' It's really beautiful and with not many tourists, quite peaceful. From the ancient medieval crypt to the second story galleries, the church houses a museum of ecclesiastical art work, stone carvings, relics, chalices, and replicas of the Hungarian Crown Jewels.

Now, I'm pretty sure Mary told us all of the information I just shared with you, plus more, about seven times. I will not repeat the previous paragraphs seven times, as I don't want to put anyone in a comatose state. But to be true to the holiday, I really should. Here goes:

Fisherman's Bastion looks like a castle and city walls, but it is a collection of terraces and towers . . . *No, I can't do it!*

We then wander through the old streets of Buda where Holly spots a tourist sporting a yellow dachshund handbag. She tries her luck with a dachshund call, but it is promptly denied.

Afterwards we cross back to the Pest side of the river to tour the Hungarian House of Parliament. It's raining, and with construction work being done outside, there are long queues and pushy tourists. It is beautiful inside, much more opulent and a lot more over the top than the Parliament House in Australia. It houses the crown of King Stephen, but honestly, the rest of the Parliament is not so interesting. I wonder if I'm running out of 'city tour steam.' I'm with the kids now and can't wait for the tour to be over. My headache is worsening by the minute.

We hop back on the bus to cross the town to the pretty City Park and through to Vajdahunyad Castle. This area on the lake's edge is so lovely, as is the castle. As we walk through the grand arched gate to the castle grounds, I can imagine a historical romance set amongst this backdrop.

Even though the walk through the park and surrounds is nice, I've turned into a grouch for the first time on the trip. A headache of epic proportions has gripped me, and even as we cross over from City Park to Heroes Square where the Kings, Queens, and Grand Dukes of Hungary are honoured, I struggle to take in any more information. Little bits of information leak in, something about the Soviet occupation and the concert held here in Heroes Square every year to commemorate their independence, but I just want to lie down.

I perk up a little afterwards when Anthony spots a dachshund out the window of the bus, a cute black miniature with a red coat. It looks so much like Charlie!

Dachshund Spotting Total:
Anthony 19, David 4, Holly 2, Mum 1, Maree 1, Lisa 1, Sam 0

I don't know what everyone else did after the tour, but I spent a few hours in bed with a migraine. I'm not exactly blaming Mary's constant chatter, but she had a way of saying everything over and over, and over, and pressing her face only a hand span from mine, awaiting a response, which I would give with a nod and/or a comment. I would step back, and she would follow, so I'd step back and she would follow again, repeating what she'd said again and again, which was all informative Budapestian information, but sometimes less is more, Mary!

The Local Remedy

I feel so much better after a rest and manage to go to our pre-booked Hungarian folklore evening and dinner. As we enter the restaurant, we are handed little porcelain pots made to look like a traditional Hungarian man, which is a keepsake of the night. In the pots is a potent Hungarian spirit that the adults sip on. Decorated with timber benches lined with sheepskin, whitewashed walls with crockery plates and jugs painted with traditional folk designs, and dark timber beams, the restaurant has a great atmosphere. While a band plays gypsy folk music, wine is poured from above the waiter's head with amazing precision from a thin tube to our glasses—without spilling a drop. For a while we wonder if we are the only patrons for the night before a stream of people fill the restaurant.

A band begins to play Hungarian folk music on the small stage before us, and before long dancers start to twirl, performing traditional folk dancing. We feast on delicious goulash soup, brought to the table in a huge pot, venison, vegetables, and strudel for dessert. Holly is not so sure about eating a reindeer though, and picks at her meat, but she's happy to eat strudel.

The best part of the evening, by far, is the folk dancing, and not only from the performers. David and Anthony are handpicked from the noisy, cheering crowd to go up on stage, followed by me, and then David again. It's hilarious! A thigh-slapping, foot-tapping dancer twirls me around the stage in a dance like the game musical chairs. The music begins, and we dance around one lone person in the middle that doesn't have a partner. Then all of a sudden the music stops, and we must switch partners quickly before we are the one left out! It's so fun. I glance over to the rest of the family. Sam, Mum, Maree, and Holly are laughing, videoing, and lying low, so they don't get picked.

The folk dancers are fantastic, and it is such a great night! I think Anthony is finally relaxing now too. Maybe all he needed was some folk dancing!

Danube Bend Tour—On a Bus

Today we leave for a big daytrip from Budapest for the Danube Bend Tour. Normally you would expect this to be *on* the Danube River, but a small downside of travelling at this time of year is that the river portion of the Danube Bend Tour is now done on a bus—with Mary, our repetitive tour guide. Honestly, she is quite nice and so friendly, but we only need to hear things once, not three or four times.

Our first stop is Esztergom about forty-five kilometres from Budapest, the one-time capital of Hungary and birthplace of King Stephen, the first king of Hungary.

We are led up the hill to the Primatial Basilica of the Blessed Virgin Mary Assumed into Heaven and Saint Adalbert, also known as the Esztergom Basilica. How's that for a name? Along with its big name, it also has the title of being the tallest building in Hungary with the cupola height measuring a hundred metres. In a modern world of skyscrapers, it's hard to believe this is the tallest building in Hungary, but Mary says it is so, several times.

The basilica is white with soaring columns and three green domes. It was built in 1856, although a small chapel has been on the site since the sixteenth century. We climb up towards the cupola to an ecclesiastical museum and treasury, containing lavish solid gold and gem-encrusted ornaments used in church services in centuries past. It also contains the largest textile collection of priest robes and embroidery in Europe, dating back to the fourteenth century, a thirteenth century book, and a crystal engraved with an image of Christ dating back to the ninth century.

I am well and truly churched out and over gem- and gold-encrusted religious items because everyone knows Jesus, a humble carpenter, needed all of this bling to show him how highly regarded he is. As does the Holy Mother, a gentle soul, happy to birth her sweet little baby in a stable. I enjoy seeing churches for history and architecture, but I am beginning to get over all the displayed wealth. I may offend some with these comments. However, faith and love of God, his Son, and the Blessed Virgin Mary is something from within, is it not? Why does this faith and love have to be shown in gold and riches? Or is this the power of the Church displaying its might? But I guess that's generally how the world operates, doesn't it? For many, showing love and faith is with material things. We are all guilty of that.

This is getting way too deep, but for me, I am happy to step out into the sunshine with the family and wander along the grounds around the basilica, high above the Danube River. We look over the view to Slovakia and the red-roofed houses of the town of Esztergom, edging the bend of the river. The kids scamper, yes, they scamper, through the trees, up stairs and rocky, ancient stones before pausing to pose for pictures before a huge twelve-metre limestone sculpture built in 2001 for the thousand-year anniversary of the coronation of King Stephen.

The tour continues to the ancient town of Visegrad to visit the ruins of a thirteenth century medieval citadel sitting high on Castle Hill overlooking, and once protecting, the Danube Bend. I am a big reader of fantasy, and it is my first love as a reader and writer, so as you can imagine, I love a castle!

Because of its strategic position, the site of Visegrad has centuries of history, from the Stone Age to the Romans to the Hungarians. The first mention of Visegrad and its fortress is in 1009. It has played a big part in Hungarian history with once being the home of the royal court and the crown jewels, and hosting the royal summit in 1335, the Congress of Visegrad, with the important kings of the time.

Although Visegrad Castle is not as restored as Trakai Castle in Lithuania, it is still steeped in history, and we all enjoy the visit. There are knights and armour, flags and pennants, feasting kings and queens, hunting scenes, and dancing lords and ladies. We pose in an ancient archway with a mini drawbridge, and Holly is locked in the stocks for the terrible crime of being cheeky.

When we arrive back to Budapest, Anthony, the kids, and I pop out for a quick walk when Anthony spots a gorgeous, brown standard dachshund. It is the biggest dachshund I've *ever* seen. It's not fat, like poor Obie the famous overweight dachshund on YouTube, but longer and broader with bigger paws, a longer neck and head, and a deeper chest. It's adorable! We don't see many of the standard size; it's usually the miniatures scampering about or large miniatures, like Charlie. We all have a pat, and it prompts some tears over Coco for Holly and me. Oh my, we miss our puppies. We talk of Coco all the way back to the apartment.

Out of the two dogs, Coco was the beggar of food. She had the perfect face for it, along with a well-timed whimper just as we were about to pop the last piece of toast into our mouths. Charlie would always sit a pace or two back, waiting patiently, his tail wagging slowly, knowing that Coco had it in the bag. As soon as food was offered, he would step forward and claim his scrap along with Coco. He would then return to his bed, but she would stay, following along wherever we walked just in case there was a miracle—like a nice juicy steak accidentally falling to the floor. Eventually though, she would give up and go find a sunny spot to lie down, usually the lounge, even though the dogs weren't allowed on the lounge. I guess rules don't apply to dachshunds . . .

It still doesn't seem real that she is gone.

Dachshund Spotting Total:
Anthony 20, David 4, Holly 2, Mum 1, Maree 1, Lisa 1, Sam 0

The Gold-Man Mystery

On our last day we go our separate ways for the day. Anthony, the kids, and I wander around the town for a couple of hours, following a tourist walk on the map. The four of us enjoy the time together, and I think it's good for Mum, Maree, and David to have their jaunts together as well. When with us, the grandparents follow our schedule, but I think it's good for them to do some exploring and see what they find. They usually become lost, but with laughter and lots of questions, they always find their way back!

We meet for lunch at a restaurant on one of the main pedestrian shopping areas in Budapest in full view of a golden-painted man, posing like a statue in the most awkward position imaginable. Sam watches the statue-man like a hawk. The golden man doesn't move or make a sound as children scamper around him and the many tourists stand watching. The awkward pose and super small size of the man have Sam convinced it's a fake. As I am writing this, it is about six days later and Sam is still trying to convince the rest of us the man was a fake as there is no way a real person could stay in that position for so long. It truly is a mystery. Will we ever know the truth?

Dinner is early tonight as we have a 6:30 pm panoramic cruise on the Danube. We pop into what we think is a cafe for a quick meal to find the most beautiful restaurant called Szazeves Etterem, the oldest restaurant in Pest, with murals painted on all the walls and stained glass windows. Holly orders sausage and chitterlings, but the waiter says they are out of that. She is quite happy about that later when we do an Internet search on chitterlings and find out they are the intestines of calves. Nice. We feasted on one of the best meals of the trip, with more schnitzel, goulash, pork loin, and veal stew in a potato pancake. Mum and I drink a Hungarian cocktail in martini glasses.

The cruise is simply outstanding. Budapest has one of the most stunning nighttime riverside panoramas I've ever seen. Thank goodness for their building boom for the thousand-year celebrations of the Hungarian State in the late 1800s, as this is spectacular.

Included with the ticket is a free drink, so we enjoy the view of beautiful Buda and Pest with a champagne, juice, and beer, and great commentary, half of which I miss as I'm constantly running outside into the cold to take pictures.

Our lovely dinner and cruise is the best finish of our visit to Budapest. I'm ready to move on because I'm looking forward to going to Cesky Krumlov in the Czech Republic. It is a tiny village and UNESCO World Heritage site that has been talked up a treat to us by Anja, a family member. Bring it on! And bring on the snow. My last weather search mentions the possibility of snow . . . O-o-o-h-h-h!

(13)

CESKY KRUMLOV, CZECH REPUBLIC

Date: November 24
Location: Budapest – Cesky Krumlov
Nights: 2
Dachshunds so far: 29

Another Fairytale Location

The van winds down towards Cesky Krumlov, crossing the bridge over the Vltava River to what is a tiny old town, nestled in a deep river bend. The bend in the river is so tight it seems like Cesky Krumlov is a little island. The van drives straight across the main square to park right in front of our hotel, the Hotel Zlaty Andel.

We check in and go to our rooms, which are through the hotel, out into a little courtyard, up and down a few sets of little stairs, and inside another building. Mum is at the bottom of the stairs in what looks like Harry Potter's room under the stairs at Privet Drive, but it's pretty, if not a bit snug. She may be referred to as 'Harry' for the remainder of the visit. Maree and David are down the hall in a lovely, big room with a full bath, and I'm cranky with myself I didn't book Mum a bigger room. Out of all the people on the holiday Mum loves her baths the most. We are upstairs in an apartment with a kitchen, two bedrooms, and a bath, and it's great to spread out. Mum books our bath for later on.

Cesky Krumlov is a gorgeous old town, and I'm so excited! It has a medieval feel to it and reminds me of Tallinn in Estonia, even if all of the buildings aren't maybe quite as old. As soon as we are checked in, we venture out for a look around the twisting cobblestone streets to get our bearings. The first thing outside the hotel is a wooden chalet selling sausage, meat, and hot mead. The name of the little stall is Svatomartinske Hody or Saint Martin's Feast. Saint Martin's Day, I am told, is a traditional feast day in the days before Advent, a feast of goose and Svatomartinské vino, the first wine from the autumn harvest. History places this feast on the eleventh of November, but I am happy that on the twenty-fourth of November there is some vino, whether it be fresh from the autumn harvest or not, for me to sip on while we stroll around the town in the late afternoon chill.

The view of the Cesky Krumlov castle from the town below is impressive. It perches high above the town on a rocky promontory, the tall bell tower looking fairytale-like with traces of pale pink and yellow on its painted exterior.

Mum and I dress for dinner early and head to the hotel bar for wine and a chat. I love relaxing with Mum in the evenings before dinner. Some time later the rest of the group joins us for dinner, but the bartender advises us that this is not the restaurant and points towards a hallway, 'Go there and turn left.'

We do that, but it leads us outside and into the courtyard below our rooms. We stand in confusion for a moment before spying a doorway down a little set of stairs. We step through into a completely empty restaurant, save a few staff, and we are seated in a booth. As we settle into our seats and look over the menu, we notice the strange artwork surrounding us. On the wall is a Picasso-style painting of a naked lady with a mousetrap on her va-jay-jay. This causes some giggling. There is also a strange mask with glasses and a condom for a nose, and a jaunty knight with a tap for a penis. We enjoy a tasty dinner amongst the interesting artwork of goulash (again!), pizza (of course), schnitzel (second favourite after pizza), pork, beef, and duck.

Oh, the Weather Outside Is—

The next day begins in an ordinary way. We get up, dress, and meet the grandparents downstairs. We let 'Harry' out of the room under the stairs (ha!) and traipse through the hotel to the breakfast room, which we can't find without asking at reception. As we're finishing up our breakfast, an extraordinary thing happens. No, it isn't a dachshund sighting. It's a snow sighting.

SNOW.

YES, it is finally snowing! Floaty white stuff! It is the first snow of our holiday, and I hope not our last. I certainly don't want any blizzards and closed-down airports, but a nice sprinkling of snow while I sip mulled wine in a Christmas market will be nice. Our first Christmas markets are in Nuremberg in a few days' time, so fingers crossed for some snow then too, and not rain or sleet or two-day-old, grey, slushy snow. I know what I want. Ha!

There is a bit of excitement from all (mostly the girls), but also Anthony, who spotted the snow first. He is claiming that not only is he the King of Dachshund Spotting, but also the King of Snow

Spotting. Breakfast is immediately abandoned (slight exaggeration), cameras are grabbed (actual event), and we race out into the cold to take pictures of us all frolicking in the snow (I wanted to use the word 'frolic'). Well, we stand and pose under the snowflakes, taking picture after picture, until one shows the faint white streak of snow.

History Lessons with Sharka

After donning the usual beanie, big jacket, gloves, and scarves, we met Sharka (that's what her name sounded like!) for a walking tour of Cesky Krumlov in the eddying snow. It begins to fall a little heavier as we cross the main square (insert excited giggling) and up the gentle slope to a lookout over the town. It may not sound that nice to do a walking tour in the snow, and for folks from the Northern Hemisphere, snow is the norm. I'm used to hot summers for Christmas, so for me, the snow adds to the holiday atmosphere and the excitement of Christmas in winter.

We duck inside Saint Vitus Church, a fourteenth century church and monastery, which has a medieval feel to it. It is all dark timbers and whitewashed walls, not the brightly painted frescoes, gold, and gilt of most churches we've seen. The organ is a beautiful centerpiece in the church.

Sharka tells us more of the turbulent history of the Czech Republic and the occupation of the country by Nazi Germany and then the Soviets. Twenty years ago, Cesky Krumlov was a rundown town in need of a huge restoration, and this could only be done after Communism. During the restoration, the layers of plaster were chipped away from the buildings to reveal frescos underneath from hundreds of years before. There are over three hundred preserved historical buildings in Cesky Krumlov. Many are original Gothic architecture but restored during the Renaissance period (sixteenth century) with murals. Each building has its own character, colour, and style.

In the sprinkling snow, we follow Sharka across the river and wind our way up to a castle, first built in the thirteenth century. Much of the castle is closed for the winter, and unfortunately we aren't able look at the Baroque Castle Theatre for which, along with the castle, Cesky Krumlov is famous. Dating back to the fourteenth century, with eighteenth century machinery, scenes, and ceiling and wall murals, it is one of the best-preserved baroque theatres in the world. It was one of the reasons why I originally picked Cesky Krumlov to visit, but the town has so much character I find I don't care.

Although the castle and theatre are closed, we still enjoy the visit, especially viewing the town from high above with the snow eddying around us. Enough has fallen now that the kids even manage to build a snowman. Or snow *person,* as Holly corrects, but in truth, it's a snow blob. However, it's the first snow blob of the holiday, and the kids pose for photos before the tiny snow person.

A Li'l Bit Loco

The town is quite hilly and meanders gently up and down, with curving narrow cobblestone streets. We pass shops with bright window displays, selling chocolate bonbons, decorations, souvenirs, jewellery, crafts, and clothes, all nestled in the lower stories of beautiful buildings decorated with sixteenth century facades with colours from blue to green to burnt orange. Restaurant railings are draped with Christmassy bushes of greenery and red berries. When we walk back to the hotel, a huge Christmas tree is being erected in the main square near it. How exciting! I don't know what it is about Christmas in Europe, but it sends me a little bit loco!

Afterwards we warm up with sausages from the Saint Martin's Feast stall, hot mead, soup, and pizza. We spend the afternoon relaxing, shopping and wandering the pretty streets of Cesky Krumlov. We're creeping closer to Christmas, and for the ladies especially, Christmas presents are on our minds. There won't be a lot this year, given we are on a trip that's costing as much as a small house, but we still like to look through the shops!

This evening we dine in a restaurant in Cesky Krumlov's town square where Sam eats the next best thing on the menu after pizza—pork schnitzel. I decide to take a risk and not order plain, *ordinary* pig, but something much more exciting—the wild boar schnitzel.

When the waiter hands it to me, he says, 'Your veal schnitzel.'

I ask, 'Boar?'

And he answers, 'Oh, yes, boar.'

Sure . . .

There is more snow in the morning when we wake, enough to cover the ground white and collect on the sloping rooflines of Cesky Krumlov's buildings. We take one more walk around the outskirts of the old town, past the mill and weir, take a few more snowy photos of the castle bell tower, and snow-capped everything. Cesky Krumlov is simply enchanting. No wonder it is a popular tourist destination, whether winter or summer.

(14)

PRAGUE, CZECH REPUBLIC

Date: *November 26*
Location: *Cesky Krumlov – Prague*
Nights: *4*
Dachshunds so far: *29*

Some Advice to Hotels

On the way to Prague, with every passing kilometre, the sky clears, the snow disappears, and we arrive to the bluest sky day we've had since Turkey, even though Weather.com assured me it might snow in Prague. Wunderground said not for a few days, so I'll stick to Weather.com until Wunderground tells me what I want to hear. I'm happy we had our snowy experience in Cesky Krumlov, but I know I'll still look on weather websites and bore the rest of the group with excited comments, like 'There is a twenty-five percent chance of snow in Nuremberg!'

At the Hotel Leonardo we come across the first hotel on the trip that provides us with everything we need to know as we check in—without one question from us!

The time of breakfast
The location of the breakfast room
The location of the lifts
A town map with tourist attractions indicated
Wi-Fi—whether or not it is free, and the code

Most hotels will tell us a combination of some of this info but never all—some give a map and tell the breakfast time, others tell the Wi-Fi code but don't offer a map.

Anthony and I have commented before that it's amazing how many hotels, as lovely as they are, only check you in and say with a smile, 'Here are your keys.' In some hotels, we are directed to where the lifts are and sometimes not. It's not always obvious where lifts are in old buildings—and the lifts in Hotel Leonardo are around a corner and down a little hallway—so not automatically easy to find.

Breakfast times vary in every hotel, but in most hotels we have to ask; they answer, but don't offer the information about where the breakfast room is, so then we ask another question. Sometimes it's on the ground floor or first floor, or as in the case of this hotel, in the basement via a different lift from the hotel room lift. In Cesky Krumlov, finding the breakfast room was like being in Hogwarts with moving staircases (OK, slight exaggeration, and we did have Harry with us, so it was OK. Ha!), but reception didn't advise where it was upon check-in, so we had to ask the first morning after wandering around for a bit.

Sensational Old Town Square

After our awesomely efficient check-in we dump our bags and head out to check out the town. I am so excited to be in Prague as I've heard so many people say it is one of their favourite European cities.

Despite the blue sky and bright sun, it's colder here in Prague, and my jacket is still not cutting it. It did get me through the snow in Cesky Krumlov, but today I'm cold. To Anthony's great excitement, I tell him all about it.

We make our way through a maze of cobblestone streets, past tourists and locals, cafes and shops. Lucky we have the map, as there doesn't seem to be a straightforward way through the surrounding streets to the square, and I don't mind at all. The alleyways are filled with shops selling everything from clothes to chocolates, replica Faberge eggs, crystal, and art. I will return.

The first thing I see as we approach Prague Old Town Square is the Gothic-looking Old Town Hall and Astronomical Clock. Decorated with a beautiful working clock, dating back to 1410, it is truly a sight to see. There are tour guides standing beneath, so we enquire as to what time the walking tours are for the following day.

The rest of the square is surrounded by Saint Nicholas Church and Tyn Church, a castle-like church with turrets and jutting spires dark against the brilliant blue sky, gorgeous Czech Baroque-style buildings of pale yellows, pinks, and blues, and shops and restaurants with Christmas decorations hanging from their awnings. White horses in red finery stand quietly before white carriages awaiting passengers. Around from the Old Town Square, food stalls sell mulled wine, ham, sausages, sauerkraut, and crepes. Although the Christmas markets are not in full swing yet, there is a small row of wooden stalls selling Christmas decorations and trinkets.

Dominating the Old Town Square is, as Buddy the Elf would put it, a ginormous Christmas tree (a real tree) being meticulously decorated by men on a cherry picker. As with Krakow and Cesky Krumlov, we are a couple of days early for the Christmas markets but extending our time in Europe would have meant missing our four days in Dublin. But now as I stand and watch the tree being decorated, I can't help but think, 'Dublin better be worth it!'

We *will* have Christmas markets in Nuremberg, Strasbourg, Paris, and London, and I have to remind myself that not everyone giggles like a little girl at the sight of a Christmas market, although the sight of a stall selling bratwurst sausages would entice an excited grin from Anthony. But all in all, despite the fact the market won't start for a few days, there is a definite Christmas feel to the Old Town Square in Prague.

We have a quick dinner that night at an Italian restaurant with more pizza, risotto, and gnocchi. Anthony had been told how cheap Czech beer was, and it is, at two Australian dollars for half a litre. A glass of water is dearer. I've heard that the Czechs are the biggest beer drinkers in the world. I wonder why!

History Lessons with Diana from Down Under

We layer on the usual cold weather gear, make our way through the narrow streets to the Old Town Square, and wait before the Old Town Hall to be allocated a guide for our walking tour. We are surprised and delighted to hear that our guide, Diana, has an Aussie accent. She explains that she was born in the Czech Republic, moved to Australia when she was a child, and returned to the Czech Republic ten years ago. It's great to hear her Aussie accent, and she is funny and friendly and, of course, working for tips. Ha!

To begin the tour we watch the medieval Astronomical Clock mark the hour. Installed in 1410, the clock is the oldest astronomical clock still working in the world. It shows the astronomical positions of the sun, moon, and zodiac. It features a calendar dial marking the months, golden Roman numerals, and a ticking hand marking the time. On the hour, moving sculptures of the Apostles rotate around the clock face, and the hooded figure of Death marches out from behind the clock to strike the hour with a sickle. Our favourite part is when a little skeleton pulls a bell with a morbid jerky hand. The big crowd around us oohs and aahs as the clock does its ancient dance. As soon as it's finished, I want to see it again. Lucky I videoed it! It's one of the best things I've seen on the trip.

We then wander through Wenceslas Square where we hear of the Czech Republic's harsh history of occupation by Nazi Germany and the Soviet Union. Diana tells us of the controversial Munich Agreement, in which a part of the former Czechoslovakia was ceded to Hitler by the powers that be in England, France, Italy, and Germany, which led to the remainder of Czechoslovakia falling into Hitler's hands for the duration of the war, an agreement Czechoslovakia was not consulted on. We hear of the Czechoslovak resistance and their assassination of the high-ranking Nazi deputy Reinhard Heydrich, of Soviet tanks storming into the city, and of how proud they are to be independent and free of tyranny.

I am humbled again as I hear these words, words that we've heard again and again as we've travelled. I can't help but feel ashamed that I didn't grasp what was happening in the world when I was younger.

I feel incredibly lucky to have grown up safely with no threat of war to my family or me. My children have grown up cared for and, I hope, a little more knowledgeable about the world than I was at their age. That's if they are listening! But I know they are, even if it's only the basics. In conversations at dinner and in our hotel room at night, Anthony and I talk to the kids about all the things we learn each day, and they do contribute to the conversation. So I know they *are* listening, in between avoiding cracks in the pavement, looking for pigeons, cats, and dogs, and asking for hot chocolate. They are learning so much about the world, more than I learned, anyway.

We follow Diana back towards the river along the pretty narrow alleyways of Prague. They are lined with shops and cafes, including a hole-in-the-wall shop selling rolled dough baked around hot rods and stuffed with toppings of your choice—Nutella, cinnamon and sugar, jam, and more. The sweet treat is called trdelnik, and the kids want one. Not wanting to stop, we assure them that we'll return after the tour, but only seconds later something else is spotted that interests all of us greatly.

Anthony spies a dachshund—and not just any dachshund. It is a cute brown puppy with a bandage on its paw, being carried by a big man in an even bigger coat. Oh . . . we want to pat it so badly, but the man is on the other side of the street and marches by quickly.

Dachshund Spotting Total:
Anthony 21, David 4, Holly 2, Mum 1, Maree 1, Lisa 1, Sam 0

We make our way through the Jewish Quarter and a Jewish cemetery. Dating back to the fifteenth century, it is the oldest cemetery in the world. It holds the remains of a hundred thousand people, all buried on top of each other in what is quite a small area. We stand before the oldest active synagogue with recorded history back to 1270 and hear how after exterminating the Jews, Hitler wanted to preserve the Jewish Quarter in Prague as a 'Museum of an Extinct Race.' It is sickening to hear.

Eventually we arrive at the centuries-old Charles Bridge and enter it through the archway of a tall Gothic tower known as Powder Gate, where the gunpowder was kept in the seventeenth century. Connecting the old town with the lesser town and castle, the bridge is a wide pedestrian avenue over the Vltava River and lined with statues.

Piggin' Out on Pig

After the tour we return to the Old Town Square and pig out on pig from the food stalls. We ask for four portions of ham, and they cut off one massive chunk and serve it to us with bread. Mum, Maree, and David have cabbage, potato, and ham in a bowl, and we crowd around a small table together and eat quickly in the cold. It is *so* good.

As if we haven't eaten enough, we then buy trdelnik stuffed with Nutella. Lucky we are doing lots of walking to work off all this food, although my coat is getting tighter and tighter.

Since it is such a beautiful clear day Anthony, the kids, and I climb the Astronomical clock tower for views over the city. It is fantastic, we haven't had many days with blue sky and the photos are so much nicer. Below is the busy old town square, the baroque buildings of the old town, church steeples, and beyond the Vltava River is the sprawl of Prague Castle. It's beautiful, and we linger, snapping photos and reading graffiti carelessly written on the ancient stone arches.

Double Trouble

Our last day is filled with shopping and exploration. There are so many narrow cobblestone streets filled with shops and boutiques tucked into alleyways and squares. Prague truly is an alluring city. We look at fake Faberge eggs, Bohemian crystal, and visit a large chocolate shop just off the square and stock up on sweet treats. I have a food disaster while eating a chicken kebab, not realising that it was dripping fatty chicken juice on the front of my winter coat the whole time I was eating it. I do not smell good.

Upon our return we hear about Maree, David, and Mum's day. They'd been gone for hours and hours, mainly because they were lost. But they laugh as they tell their tale of their adventurous walk to the Jewish Quarter in the wrong direction, but with a little help from a friendly receptionist in a hotel, they find their way back. They looked through a synagogue, walked across Charles Bridge for lunch, and although they got terribly lost, they had a wonderful time. And the best thing of all? Maree had a double dachshund sighting and shows us her photographic evidence of our first smooth haired, dapple coloured dachshund! Awesome spotting!

Dachshund Spotting Total:
Anthony 21, David 4, Maree 3, Holly 2, Mum 1, Lisa 1, Sam 0

Close Call

I head out on my own one last time in the afternoon as I want to have some time to stroll and look at what I want to look at when I want to look at it, which doesn't always happen in a group. A man approaches as I walk along the street our hotel is located on, which is not anything peculiar. But as he comes closer, he begins to yell and crosses the road towards me. I look around, but the street is quiet. The few restaurants are not open yet, and I cannot see anyone in either direction. I try to sidestep him, but he grabs at me, one hand on my arm, the other reaching around me. I scream in his face and break away, but he grabs me again, this time on my backside, so I begin to run, but not before he grabs at me one more time. I run all the way to Charles Bridge where there are crowds of tourists.

I am shaking all the way to the Old Town Square and sit down for a while to watch the wooden stalls of the Christmas market being erected. I buy a coffee and linger amongst the crowds of the square until I feel OK. I force myself to wander through the shops, not wanting to allow the experience to ruin my outing. I'm glad I did as I find a beautiful crystal dachshund to give to Anthony for his birthday.

When I return to the hotel, I am cautious as I turn down the street that leads to the hotel. It is busy with tourists, but I know after a hundred metres or so, it will be quiet. The farther I get, I see that it is a little busier now, but I walk quickly, with an eye out for that horrible man. It's not a nice way to finish my time in Prague, but our delicious dinner eaten at the Bavarian food stalls on the square almost makes up for it. The markets are almost ready to start and by the looks of it, they will be beautiful.

NUREMBERG, GERMANY

Date: *November 30*
Location: *Prague – Nuremberg*
Nights: *2*
Dachshunds so far: *32*

In It to Win It

S am finally enters the competition by spotting a brown, longhaired dachshund from the van as we leave Prague. It is a lightening-fast spotting, like his dad. He's been saying for weeks that he didn't care if he saw one or not, and that he would auction the sighting off to the highest bidder. But right now, he is super excited and on a mission to beat Holly, and only Holly, who is on two.

Dachshund Spotting Total:
Anthony 21, David 4, Maree 3, Holly 2, Mum 1, Lisa 1, Sam 1

Our hotel rooms aren't ready when we arrive to Nuremberg, but I'm eager to see our first Christmas market. After missing them by only days in Krakow, Cesky Krumlov, and Prague, I'm more than a little excited.

We walk across the road and pass through the ancient city walls. They are high, with even higher defense towers that loom above what was once the moat surrounding the city. The moat, now a lovely park, also seems to be a lair for long-bodied dogs, as Sam spots another dachshund racing along with owner in tow. There is some heckling from Sam about catching up to Holly.

Dachshund Spotting Total:
Anthony 21, David 4, Maree 3, Holly 2, Sam 2, Mum 1, Lisa 1

Careful What You Wish For

Under Anthony's direction, we enter the old town and turn right. Before long we reach a beautiful little market inside what looks like a courtyard within the city walls. But we don't stay long, as I'm excited beyond normal reasoning about the Nuremberg markets, one of Germany's most famous Christmas markets. Unbeknownst to Anthony, the *whole entire trip* had been changed around so I—ahem, I mean—*we* could go to these markets.

All the way down the busy street leading to the main square, smaller markets are set up and buildings, light posts, and shopfronts are draped with Christmas decorations. Up ahead there is a man dressed in a Santa suit busking. A little dog sits on his shoulder in his own doggy Santa suit, luring in the children, so parents feel they need to drop money in his open guitar case.

The closer we come to the Christmas market, the more crowded it becomes. The only thing I can see, other than the slanting green roofline of rows and rows of wooden market stalls, is people. Thousands of them. And, in all of these crowds Anthony manages to spot a brown dachshund trotting along in a cute blue coat. The Christmas markets are forgotten briefly as we watch it pass us by.

Dachshund Spotting Total:
Anthony 22, David 4, Maree 3, Holly 2, Sam 2, Mum 1, Lisa 1

The markets are so busy we can hardly walk. It's packed and noisy—one of those situations where people need to link arms, or they will be separated. I am in Christmas market Hell. Where are the lovely markets I remember from our last European jaunt? Where are the people casually wandering arm in arm, drinking mulled wine, with a dreamy Christmassy look in their eyes while snow drifts around them? Where is it? Tell me now!

As you can imagine, it took the shine off my first Christmas market of the holiday.

We slowly make our way through, but it's like moving through a mosh pit at a concert. It appears arriving to Nuremberg on the opening weekend of the market is not a good idea. The market goes for a month, so do not, I repeat—do not go for the opening of the market. Wait a day or two. Or three.

As we press through, I see food, crafts, and decorations from a distance, and it's *so* not fun. Not fun at all. We manage to squeeze through to the end where it's a little quieter and buy lunch, three little sausages on a bread roll. We eat them as we wander back to the hotel, hoping our rooms are ready. The sausages are called Nurnburger rostbratwurst, a tiny sausage that Nuremberg is known for. And they are *so* good, especially when loaded up with sauerkraut and mustard. I think we all could have eaten another one. You may have noticed there are no vegetarians on this trip.

Second Time's a Charm

After checking in to our hotel, Mum, Holly, and I go back down to the old town while Anthony goes to the gym, Sam writes in his holiday diary (snort of laughter), I mean plays his Nintendo DS, and Maree and David have a cup of tea. I, for one, want to try and have another look at the markets without a group of seven people. I also need to find the elusive perfect jacket, which has become more urgent, as not only am I cold, but while eating that tasty kebab in Prague, the chicken fat that dripped down my front has permeated every fibre of the jacket. Plus, even though I washed it, the aroma of Lisa is now undeniably of chicken fat, more importantly, the distinct aroma of chicken kebab meat. And while I admit that the distinguished and beloved dachshunds of the world must find me intoxicating, those of the human sort are not so impressed.

No luck with the jackets again as they are all way too dear, but we buy chocolate. There is no evidence left, so it cannot be proven. Grandma said there was no chocolate, and all grandmas are trustworthy. Everyone knows that.

It isn't as busy near the markets this time, and I realise that earlier we may have turned up at the beginning of the day's trading. I breathe a sigh of relief when I see it is much quieter now. Taking our time, the three of us take a wander up and down the rows of chalets with hundreds of handmade, locally produced goodies for us to look at.

With over two hundred stalls, the Nuremberg Christmas Market dates back to the 1600s. Now that we can see it—it's bright and colourful and so festive! There is lebkuchen, a sweet gingerbread, and prune people made from dried prunes, figs, and walnuts that

147

are dressed up in many different guises—but they are not for eating, decoration only. There are decorated biscuits, chocolate-covered fruit, roasted nuts, pretzels, candles, Christmas decorations, and every miniature thing imaginable for dollhouses. Stalls sell mulled wine in souvenir mugs, sausages, pork, potato fritters, and crepes. Every stall is decorated with boughs of greenery. It is a nice way to spend the afternoon and a much nicer introduction to the markets than earlier.

Willkommen to the Eurozone

We enjoy a dinner of schnitzel, potato, beef, soup, and pasta, and we pay for our first dinner in euros. To say that David is relieved to arrive in the Eurozone is an understatement. The constant currency changes have been something of a frustration for him, so he feels much more comfortable now. We've had Singapore dollars, Turkish lira, Russian rubles, a quick euro for two days in Estonia, then Latvian lats, Lithuanian lits, Polish zloty, the Hungarian forint, and the Czech koruna. There are still British pounds and US dollars to go. It has been the most changes of currency we've ever had on a holiday.

Mum, Holly, and I wander back, *yet again*, to look at the Christmas market and night-lights of Nuremberg. It's right then I remember that I've forgotten to purchase an essential piece of Christmas-ness. An Advent calendar!

How could I have forgotten? It is the first of December tomorrow, and I don't have a calendar! How will we know what day of December it is? How will the kids receive their Advent gifts without it? Despite a lengthy search, I can't find a calendar at the markets, but I buy a Christmas tree decoration and lose an expensive glove.

For You, My Little Monkeys

The next day is, of course, the first of December, and although there is no festive calendar, we work out what date it is, and Advent still goes ahead. Advent for the kids equals chocolate, treats, or gifts, which I usually hide. To find them, they must solve a Christmas-inspired riddle or sing Christmas carols. Dance monkeys, dance!

Today they must sing the first line of 'The Twelve Days of Christmas' and after a not-so-tricky clue, find the hidden gift in the hotel room, which today is a Christmas tree decoration. The search for the gift takes about ten seconds. This was much more fun when they were younger. I explain that for Advent on Christmas Eve, they must sing the whole song for an extra special gift.

'What gift?' they want to know.

'It's a surprise,' I reply. I have no idea, though!

History Lessons with Elizabeth

We meet Elizabeth, our guide, for the longest walking tour in the history of walking tours. I've failed the group as tour director. Two hours is a great walking tour, three hours is pushing it. But four hours? It's not the actual walking that's the problem; four hours is simply too long. Plus, at six weeks into the trip, we've perhaps had enough of walking tours. Having said that, we *do* enjoy seeing more of what is a beautiful medieval town. We learn of Nuremberg's long history, dating back to the year 1050, its strategic position in the region, the ancient city walls, and the six-kilometre moat circling the city, the only German city that still has one.

We are taken through an artisan's market, past a twelfth century tower house with bullet holes marring its facade from World War Two, and then on to the Holy Ghost Hospital, a fourteenth century centre for the sick and elderly. The hospital, along with ninety percent of the buildings in the old town, were severely damaged in bombing raids by the Allied Forces in World War Two and took twenty years to rebuild. We walk along the Pegnitz River, over arching bridges, including a medieval covered bridge, before wandering down a street full of medieval, half-timbered buildings. As we walk, a gorgeous carriage drawn by draught horses clip-clops down the cobblestones past us.

At the Christmas market we all grab a quick snack of potato fritters and a piece of chocolate-covered lebkuchen, a gingerbread made from a special recipe dating back six hundred years. I hate gingerbread and all things ginger, yet I like this. It leads me to think that there is no ginger in there at all.

Sam is keeping on top of his schoolwork by completing three months of community service by helping his Grandma and Nonna up hills. Arms linked, the three walk up the hill slowly behind the rest of us as we make our way up the sloping streets to Nuremberg Castle. He won't be happy if I make him do a reflection like they do at school!

Sam, how did it make you feel to help two old ladies walk up a hill?

Explain how your view of the world has improved by helping two old ladies up hills for three months.

What would you do differently now that you've practiced it many times?

What are the risks involved with helping two old ladies walk up a hill?

Farther up the hill is Kaiserburg, or Nuremberg Castle. Once this castle was one of the most important in Europe, the seat of Holy Roman Emperors and the meeting place of kings, dukes, and important dignitaries. Sitting high above the town, it offers a great viewing point over Nuremberg. The castle is a series of buildings, towers, and courtyards that we wander around slowly, mingling with the tourists at the lookout and peering over the town below. Elizabeth points out a building in the distance where 'Hitler made his famous speech.' So far on the walking tour, there has been no talk of World War Two other than the damage to the town by the Allied Forces.

The fact World War Two is not mentioned may not have seemed strange if this were the start of our holiday. But having travelled through Estonia, Latvia, Lithuania, Poland, Budapest, Cesky Krumlov, and the Czech Republic, and heard stories of tyranny and terror from Nazi Germany in World War Two, then to arrive to Nuremberg and hear not one word about it other than, 'Over there is where Hitler made his famous speech,' to me is a little odd.

The tour would have seemed more balanced had there been the occasional mention of World War Two. History is history, and although Nuremberg is a town with a rich history and an awesome Christmas market, it was central to many events that occurred during the war, and I was interested in hearing more about it.

The kids are *so* relieved the walking tour is over that it's not funny. The four hours were like a hundred in their minds. They are appeased by the fact that it is the last booked walking tour on the trip. I don't mention that there may be more, but I haven't booked them yet. That is a chat for later!

Anthony and I talk of visiting the Documentation Centre Nazi Rally Grounds in the afternoon, (without the kids—I think they would have divorced us had we tried to take them), but we only have two nights in Nuremberg, and this is our last afternoon here. We decide we want to fill it with enjoyment. The smell of sizzling sausages, potato fritters, and roasted nuts fill our noses, so we return to the Christmas market to fill our bellies with Nuremberg's finest market fare. And it's good.

Another Tight Squeeze

At the end of the market is the queue for the horse and carriage rides. We all decide to go on one, even me after the sneeze fest carriage ride in Krakow. That I am allergic to horses, or horsehair, is an understatement, but I'm in a glorious yellow filled-in carriage with Christmassy trim. I figure if I am sitting inside, the horsiness won't infiltrate my senses. I was wrong. The sneezing, runny nose, and watery eyes commence within minutes.

The carriage is perhaps too small for seven people, and although the children are aged twelve and fifteen, they are pretty much the size of adults. Holly is on Anthony's lap, and we are all squished so tightly, we're more cuddling than sitting next to each other. We assure the man we are comfortable, but we are not. We are taken around Nuremberg along cobblestone streets and alleyways and past gawking onlookers who, like us when we saw the carriage go by, must be thinking, 'We might have to do that.' We laugh and joke in the close quarters of the carriage and pose for goofy photos.

As we walk back through the old town to the hotel, there is a call of 'Dachshund!' as Holly spots an adorable dachshund being carried in a handbag. Holly and I talk about Coco, how she would have loved to have been a handbag dog if she'd been given the chance.

Mum and I are equal at last place. But I am really and truly last, as she saw her dachshund first.

Dachshund Spotting Total:
Anthony 22, David 4, Maree 3, Holly 3, Sam 2, Mum 1, Lisa 1

Back at the hotel, after a Google search, I find out there *is* a separate World War Two tour of Nuremberg, which sounds really interesting, but I still think basically ignoring the fact that World War Two even happened in a four-hour walking tour of Nuremberg is a little odd.

That evening the adults buy mulled wine, or gluhwein, at the market in mugs we can keep. It is hot and sweet, and I wrap my cold hands around the mug and sip it as we walk to dinner. I don't know why wandering in the cold and drinking mulled wine at Christmas makes me giddy. But it just does! We pass the children's Christmas market with its two-story carousel and Santa Claus' house. I insist on buying two red beanies for the kids that are way too small for their heads and would be a more appropriate size for a five-year-old. Hmmm. Nice keepsake though!

The restaurant of choice is Oberkrainer, a traditional German restaurant on the corner of the Hauptmarkt, which is a contender for the favourite restaurant of the trip. We are led upstairs to our own little private dining booth and proceed to order a whole lotta pork—pork schnitzel, pork sausage, pork shoulder with the best crackling, pork steak, and potato dumplings and fries. Dad would have loved it.

France, here we come!

(16)

STRASBOURG, FRANCE

Date: *December 2*
Location: *Nuremberg — Strasbourg*
Nights: *2*
Dachshunds so far: *36*

The Patience of a Saint

The day begins with a riddle and room search for an Advent gift. I wasn't quite prepared this morning, so before they wake, I scribble out a few woeful non-Christmassy clues. The first of which is, 'Look where my clothes are.' Riddle *that*, kids!

It leads them to my suitcase and a little wooden Christmas tree with tiny decorations that, as mentioned in the next note, 'must be put together without fighting.'

Did they quite get the Christmas tree together without a small fight? The answer—*no*. I have a video highlighting that two siblings working together is almost impossible, especially when the older one takes charge and barely lets the younger one help. Intervention by parent is required.

After the tree is put together, we then subsequently pull it apart, so we can pack it in the suitcase. I start to laugh when I realise what a stupid thing this was to buy, especially when the twenty-four little wooden tree decorations fall out of the box and scatter to the floor.

When I see Anthony's small smile, I know it doesn't surprise him that I bought a wooden tree that needs disassembling every time we move on. I admit I do buy silly things while travelling, like deciding shot glasses would be the perfect keepsake from every city on our previous trip. After buying glasses in Santorini and Athens with thirty-three cities ahead of us, Anthony rightly pointed out that maybe shot glasses were not the best thing to collect. And do we even drink shots? No.

On the same trip I bought patches, embroidered badges depicting each city in every single place we went to. My plan was to sew each on a big banner for the kids to hang in their rooms once we returned home. Has this memento of epic proportions been made? No. Where are the patches now, several years later? I don't know.

Does my husband sometimes have the patience of a saint? Yes.

Another Layer of Magic

After another pack-up and check-out, we're picked up and taken on a winding road trip from Nuremberg to Strasbourg in France. Just across the border from Germany, Strasbourg is a town of both German and French influences. It is the seat of the European Union and, more importantly, hosts an epic Christmas market of over three hundred market chalets in eleven sites around the town. The Strasbourg market, founded in 1570, hosts the oldest known Christmas market. Admittedly, the town is also famous for a few other features, including its architecture and the winding canals of Petite France, a UNESCO World Heritage Site.

The town looks absolutely gorgeous as we drive in, and as soon as we dump our bags in what is a huge apartment-style hotel room in La Maison Rouge Hotel, we set off. It's so cold outside, I vow that I will not leave this town without a new jacket. The chicken fat smell is not going anywhere, I'm shivering, and although I can't fit another layer underneath my jacket, I still secretly hope for some snow to add another layer of magic to what is already a magical place.

After a map check, our first walk is to the Strasbourg Cathedral. On the way little wooden market chalets dot the walkways, and beneath the towering Gothic cathedral lies a small square with a festive market, the Marche de Noel de la Cathedrale.

The chalets are full of beautiful arts and crafts, and Christmas decorations. One chalet is completely dedicated to Santa hats. There is the smell of sweet crepes and sausages sizzling on hot plates, and a band is busking under the first floor overhang of Maison Kammerzell, a medieval, half-timbered building. The square and narrow streets are filled with so many Christmas decorations it's almost kitschy. Take my word for it—the town of Strasbourg is *very* festive.

We stroll down from the cathedral past more markets and decorated buildings to the Ile River for a tour around the old city in a glass-top boat. After purchasing our tickets for the Batorama canal cruise, a long canal boat pulls up, and soon enough we are filing onboard and grabbing headphones for the audio tour.

With the glass-top roof, it's definitely a warmer canal cruise than in St. Petersburg. We glide under bridges and past narrow, half-timbered houses with deeply sloping rooflines. The medieval buildings are firmly reinforced by centuries-old dark timbers, but there is a slight slant to all the buildings, which suggests they all seem to be holding each other up. Soon we are floating past the Saint Thomas Church and to an area known as Petite France, named a UNESCO World Heritage site for its medieval houses. In the Middle Ages, fisherman, millers, and tanners set up shop here, and now these historic old buildings draw tourists from all over the world.

Anthony, otherwise known as Eagle Eyes, has a double dachshund sighting from the boat, startling a few other tourists with his call. All thoughts of Petite France and the voice coming through our headphones are immediately abandoned as we all crane our necks in the tight rows of seating to see them. I try, without success, to take a photo of two of the cutest miniature dachshunds. Scampering along, they both bark at a passer-by like true dachshunds.

Dachshund Spotting Total:
Anthony 24, David 4, Maree 3, Holly 3, Sam 2, Mum 1, Lisa 1

FYI on the Mighty Dachshund

Maree and David's last pair of dachshunds, Sam and Blacky, were non-barkers. Who would have thought such dachshunds existed? But they do!

I grew up with Pancho II, who would bark from his kennel in the back yard. I have so many memories of Dad hollering, 'SHUT UP!' out the back door I can still hear it now. And as for Pancho III and Pepe, Anthony's and my first pair? Barking was a fun and all-consuming activity for them.

Is that a bird? BARK! Is there a car within a five-kilometre radius? BARK! Did I step in the vicinity of where the dog food is kept? BARK! Is the sky blue? BARK!

Pancho II was also a hater of all things feline, and with a case of small-dog syndrome, he often thought that taking on the German shepherd guard dogs in the property across the road was a great idea. How he survived, I don't know. He was quite territorial with Mum, but only if he was on her lap. If my sister, Karen, and I tried to show Mum *any* affection at all, or even approach her, he would growl. Thinking it was the best game ever, I would go backwards and forwards to hear him growl each time. Of course, it would end with him snapping at me. But regardless of this, he was an affectionate, hilarious dog who will always be my first dachshund.

Dachshunds are friendly, affectionate, playful, inquisitive, lazy, and loyal. They are also a little naughty, think they are bigger than they actually are, good at stealing sandwiches from tabletops four times their height, and capable of carefully unwrapping a box of chocolates and sampling a few. They are also good at begging, leaving the occasional turd in a not-often-used room in a house, and are exceptionally talented at going through bags of garbage stacked up after a party. It's always so nice to wake up with a hangover to massacred garbage bags and food scraps spread across the back patio.

As a breed that is very much into its food, we once found Pepe with his head stuck inside a bag of dry dog food. And Coco would beg for things she didn't even like! We have a video of her begging for leaves of baby spinach. Each one we give to her, she spits out and immediately begs for another and another. It makes us laugh every time we watch it.

The only conclusion I can come up with is that dachshunds must always be in a constant state of survival or in 'fight or flight' mode. If there is food, they *must* have it. But they *are* hunters and originally were bred for pursuing and killing burrowing animals, like badgers, foxes, hares, and other small prey. They are tenacious and very courageous, some almost to the point of foolishness, like Pancho II taking on a German shepherd guard dog, or Coco with a venomous snake.

Each dachshund I see on the holiday reminds me about losing Coco, but it also makes me think of *all* the dachshunds we've loved, and there have been many through three generations of families. Each one has left us with so many cherished memories that will never leave us.

'How about I organise another Skype date with Charlie?' I suggest to Holly as the boat leads us away from the two dachshunds. It's time to see our boy again.

Extreme Festivity

By the time we return it's just becoming dark, so we take another walk around the town. It is now, as night approaches, that Strasbourg's Christmas atmosphere truly shines. Decorations drape from half-timbered, medieval buildings and lampposts, and stretch across narrow walkways. The balcony of one house is decked out with reindeer, polar bears, Christmas trees, teddy bears, and more. Another has gingerbread men hanging from long red ribbons. Lights are strung above, back and forth, between the buildings. Green bushes with red berries decorate shopfronts and restaurants, and reindeer, candy canes, and oversized baubles and stars hang from sparkly string.

Along the way, market stalls and small shops line the narrow walkway, and we buy Anthony a festive singing snowman tie. I am also convinced by my clever daughter *not* to buy a standing dachshund timber jigsaw puzzle, which is almost as big as a real dachshund.

Hand in hand with Anthony, we make our way through the town until we come to Place Kleber, a large square with a ginormous Christmas tree, the biggest one we've seen so far. It has a miniature village with brightly lit windows at its base. Known as the Sharing Village, the marketplace has huts of charitable groups and a place to drop off gifts for the needy.

Seconds later we are drawn away from the tree by the sound of loud music, and an amazing light and music show begins on the side of a long building bordering the square. To the sounds of children singing 'Silent Night' in French, a train choo-choos along the building, followed by trumpets and the whisper voice at the beginning of singer Bjork's famous song 'Quiet.' Jumping gingerbread men caper across the building when the song becomes loud. We watch Superman-themed gaming, lullabies, dancing ballerinas, and a marching band crossing the building facade in time to 'All You Need Is Love.' We stand together against the cold and watch every second of it. It is fantastic!

After our walk, we all dine in a restaurant nestled along a beautiful street surrounding Petite France. We enjoy spaghetti bolognaise, pork schnitzel, cordon bleu, vegetables, and bread pretzels. It is a huge feast served by a friendly waiter.

We're enjoying the festive feel of Strasbourg and the talk turns to Christmas in New York City and how excited the rest of the family must be at home. My sister, her husband, and their kids have already left, road tripping through California, Nevada, and the central USA to New Orleans before returning to Washington. The others, Anthony's two siblings, Chris and Gemma, are preparing to leave with their families, as are our best friends, Heidi and Anthony and their kids, for weeks of travel before meeting us.

I still can't believe we've managed to pull this off—meeting all the family in New York City for Christmas—while the children are still young and grandparents young enough to enjoy what really is a once-in-a-lifetime holiday. I love the trip, as does everyone, but the pull of family and kinship niggles inside all of us, and it's exciting to think we'll see everyone soon. What an epic trip this has turned into, and all of this grew from the passing of my dad.

I notice the Christmas vibe in Nuremberg and Strasbourg has distracted Holly from being so homesick. It has distracted me as well from my grief over Coco's death. It happened so close to the trip that again and again, I often forget she is gone. It was much like this when Dad passed, as it is for all who are left behind when someone dies. When they are not here, for a few moments every day, you can almost think they are in fact not dead, the mind so connects to what once was that it slips up.

Packed Full of Delight

For Advent this morning the kids need to say a quote from the best Christmas movie of all time, *Elf*, starring Will Ferrell. Who can come up with the best quote?

Holly: We're going to eat sugarplums, go ice-skating, and maybe even hold hands!

Sam: I'm in a store, and I'm singing. I'm in a store, AND I'M SINGING.

Now according to Sam, Holly's quote is not correct, but Sam did not sing, even though clearly he should have—but what can I say? They're cute, so after a few attempts to get Sam to sing, I give them their chocolate reindeers, which are promptly eaten.

Sam, Holly, and I go ice-skating while Anthony, Maree, David, and Mum watch for a while. It's a small rink, but we have it to ourselves for most of the time, and we skate for about half an hour. It is fun, and we all get to see Sam's awesome skating skills, so lucky us.

Afterwards I *finally* buy a new jacket. It's not exactly what I want as I don't look awesomely fashionable, along the lines of model Derek Zoolander. I appear more like a dark, wintery blob, but it's the right price and it's warm and soft. My old coat has a fitting ending to its life and is stuffed in the bin!

Lunch of crepes, pretzels, and fresh rolls is eaten as we begin our self-guided audio walking tour. The kids, not impressed, hold their audio guides to their ears obediently, but I suspect there is not much listening going on. Organised in the tourist office near the cathedral, for five euros, it's a cheap way to learn more about Strasbourg.

Our first stop is the Strasbourg Cathedral, and even though I am over-churched on the holiday, I do like this one with its eighteen-metre high astronomical clock. Similar to the one in Prague, its parts are synchronised to move at different times of the day. These parts include angels, the Apostles, and Death, as well as the days of the week, the zodiac, and the phases of the moon. It is a wonder of ancient mechanics.

Farther along the kids play in a park, and we see a half-timbered house decorated with what I think are Smurfs. However, on closer inspection I realise they are polar bears with bright blue presents, an easy mistake I think, but others in the group don't think so! Wandering down narrow streets and through squares, we pass a Christmas market along the way, and David takes a photo of the Rotary rubber ducky overlooking the Ile River.

As the tour winds up, there's a loud dachshund call from Sam. We all turn to see a scruffy wirehaired dachshund. It's adorable!

Sam and Holly are now neck and neck in the competition. I am still last!

Dachshund Spotting Total:
Anthony 24, David 4, Maree 3, Holly 3, Sam 3, Mum 1, Lisa 1

Waving bye to the group, Holly and I wander off for some mum-and-daughter time and Christmas shopping. We also need to rectify the Advent calendar situation, so we don't have a third December day without a visual countdown to Christmas. After much searching, we finally find a massive Santa face for five euros with little pockets for each day of December in Santa's beard. A little string with a snowflake attached moves to show each day.

Around the corner from the cathedral is a carousel, and Holly and I can't resist a ride. When we buy our tickets, the ticket seller looks at us a little oddly before telling us 'to make sure we go on the horses only' and not the other parts of the ride. Holly and I nod, thinking he is telling us because the horses are *way* more fun. But no, we realise when we settle ourselves on the quite small horses with our knees up near our chins that the carousel is meant for small children only, and Holly and I are a little bit too big for it— even on the horses. We are the only ones on the carousel, and we giggle the whole time.

After a takeaway dinner in the room, Anthony and I take a late evening wander to see the Christmassy sights of Strasbourg one more time. What a beautiful town!

PARIS, FRANCE

Date: *December 4*
Location: *Strasbourg – Epernay – Paris*
Nights: *3*
Dachshunds so far: *39*

Chez Champers

We are picked up early today for the 342-kilometre drive to Epernay, in the Champagne region for a tour of the cellars of Moet and Chandon. The tour begins in the original home of Claude Moet, who established the house in 1743. The expansive and beautiful home sits on the Avenue de Champagne amongst the other prestigious champagne houses of the region.

Through its 270-year history the house has been visited by an emperor, kings, tsars, and dukes, and has a royal warrant to supply champagne to Queen Elizabeth II. We also learn Dom Perignon, the most famous of all champagnes, named after a Benedictine monk who pioneered sparkling wine, is made at the house of Moet and Chandon.

I follow the guide down into the cellars to twenty-eight kilometres of tunnels and rumored millions of bottles. It is dark and damp and has that musty earthy smell all cellars have. At times there are low, roughly hewn ceilings curving above us and at other times high, lofty, and neatly bricked ceilings. We pass by racks and racks of dusty bottles of Moet and Chandon. They rest quietly in the tunnels and arched alcoves, hushed like sleeping babies that should not be disturbed. They will be ready, in good time, to be enjoyed by the champagne lovers of the world.

His Favourite City

It's a relatively quick run to Paris and our apartments, La Maison Saint Germain, in the Latin Quarter of Paris. Situated on the left bank of the Seine, the lovely apartments are surrounded by shops, patisseries, restaurants, and Christmas cheer, but possibly the best thing of all is the washing machine.

'There shall be clean clothes,' sayeth the Lord, 'and it was good.'

It's dusk, and we're ready for the culinary delights of the Paris Christmas Market—bratwurst, pork, or ham on a roll, which will be eaten quickly in the cold with gloves off. On our previous trip, when it was minus twelve degrees Celsius and snowing, I came up with the grand plan of eating our dinner at the Munich Christmas Market. It was all wonderful until the chilly temperatures made it nearly impossible to eat food with our gloves off. I learned my lesson, but it isn't anywhere close to being that cold tonight. In fact, it's probably around five degrees Celsius, so almost balmy in comparison.

I start piling on the winter gear, a process that, out of everyone, always takes me the longest. I'll manage to put my gloves on before zipping up my coat or my scarf won't stay in the right spot or I need to dash to the toilet. You'd think I'd have this sorted by now. It's much the same when Anthony and I go for a ride on the Ducati at home. How many times can one woman put her gloves on before zipping her jacket or doing up the sash on the helmet? The answer for Lisa: infinity times.

As we depart, all of us filing out of the apartment building to the busy Boulevard Saint Germaine, I grin at Anthony and he grins back. It's so exciting to be in Paris!

As we cross the Pont Neuf Bridge, Anthony comments that Paris is his favourite city. Mum and I exchange a look at this comment from Anthony, and I hold in a big laugh. I swear that when I put Paris on the itinerary, he responded, 'I've already been to Paris—I want to go to different places on this trip.'

It took some sneaky itinerising (it's a word—I know it is) to extend the stop at Paris from 0 days, to 2 days, to 3 and then 4, without Anthony noticing. I took full advantage of the fact that he was busy at work and didn't have time to go over the itinerary. I thought we'd get here, and he'd declare, 'Why are we staying four nights in Paris? We've already been here.' But no, he takes a deep, in-drawn breath, glances around at the wonder of Paris, and remarks, 'Paris is my favourite city.'

I haven't planned much in Paris as we have all been before, including Maree, David, and Mum, all in the same year but on different trips, so we've seen the usual first-time visitor sights. As Anthony will agree, the City of Light is definitely a place to return to, again and again. We only have four nights here this time, but already, having only been here an hour, I wish we were staying longer.

Pausing in the centre of Paris's oldest bridge, we look to the night-lights for a few minutes and the sparkling Eiffel Tower, shining a beam of light across the sky. On the right bank is the Louvre and beyond it the slowly turning lights of a sixty-metre high Ferris wheel in the gardens of the Place de la Concorde. Beyond that is the long stretch of Christmas fanfare following the length of the Champs-Elysees with the curve of the Arc de Triomphe far in the distance. There is more light, of course, the city practically shines, reflecting in the Seine beneath us, as does the huge turning circle of the Ferris wheel. I draw in a deep breath and hold it there. I don't know what it is about Paris, but it is just so . . . *Paris*. Only a writer can explain something so well, I'm sure.

Mais Non, Madame

As we leave the bridge and cross to the Right Bank, the talk turns to the last time we were here when we encountered one of the 'ring ladies' who surreptitiously drop a gold ring at the feet of a passing tourist and then exclaim she has found your lost ring. You then say it is not your ring—*because it isn't*—and the ring lady follows with something along the lines of, 'No, I insist you must have it, but can you pay me a little for this expensive gold ring?'

They then expect you to hand over money for a crappy gold-plated ring that you've seen them put at your feet. It is beyond my ability to comprehend how people fall for this, and we wonder if we'll see a ring lady—and sure enough, minutes later, we do. The couple she approaches is onto her, however, and they send her on her way.

I don't mind going along with 'Let me shine your shoes' and then being hit up for cash, or getting a picture with a gladiator in front of the Coliseum and then being hit up for cash because even though it's a bit of a trick on unsuspecting tourists, you do get something out of it—shiny shoes and a photo with a gladiator. Even David with his epic haircut in Kusadasi did indeed look ten years younger after his added beauty treatments. But the ring ladies, this one is pure scam.

More of the Good Life

We walk along the length of the Louvre Museum, through the decorated gardens of the Jardin des Tuileries, and past the slowly turning Ferris wheel. People gather at its base, lining up for tickets, and beyond, in a long, glittering avenue is the beginning of the Marche de Noel, the Paris Christmas Market.

The Champs Elysees looks magical from this vantage point. White gable-roofed market stalls line each side with brightly lit decorations hanging from light posts, trees, and stalls. High above, a sleigh and reindeer zoom from side to side over the busy street. We join the throng of people, past ice sculptures and food stalls selling sizzling sausages, mulled wine, and gingerbread. And if there is a stall selling mulled wine, then chances are I will buy it. Before long, Mum, Maree, and I order a glass each, warm our hands that clutch the toasty mugs, and pose for a photo together. I snuggle in between my two mums. I'm glad we're all together for this journey.

We walk up and down both sides of the Champs Elysees, grab dinner on the go—hot chips, bratwurst, and crepes—and look through the stalls. The market is beautiful, exciting, and magical, and the Champs-Elysees practically glows with Christmas cheer, but the contents of the market stalls are not particularly Christmassy. They're not like the ones in Nuremberg and Strasbourg, and I guess the Bavarian-style Christmas markets are what I'm used to. Most of the Parisian stalls are filled with jewellery, hats, scarves, and general stuff that can be found anywhere, at anytime of the year.

But regardless, I love it, it's sparkly and Christmassy, and I'm drinking mulled wine while ambling arm in arm with Anthony and Holly. The only thing missing is some light snow. Sam wanders ahead with David to check out the ice-skating rink.

'Can we go ice-skating?' Sam asks.

But before Anthony or I can answer, Holly chimes in with, 'Can we go on the Ferris wheel too?'

Yes and yes. Life is good.

Divine Brekkie

After a sleep-in, the kids race up and down the narrow staircase in the apartment, completing a scavenger hunt for their treat of a Kinder Surprise Santa Claus. I leave them to put together their Kinder toys before heading out to buy breakfast. And no, they are not five and seven years of age, but twelve and fifteen. Kinder toys are fun at any age, it seems.

I'm looking for dachshunds as I walk, hoping I'll see one out for a morning stroll. I want to see one *so* badly it plays on my mind. Stupid, I know. It's not like spotting a sausage dog in Paris at 9 am in the morning will bring Coco back, but I want to see one. *Me* spot one—not somebody else. We're half way through the trip, and I've only spotted one. I miss Charlie and Coco so much, much more than I would've had Coco not died. But she did, and I cannot think about her without tearing up. Coco was my girl. Everyone in the family loved her, and she loved everyone. However, as I work from home, the dogs are a big part of my day. It was so strange in those few days after Coco. It was quiet, we were quiet. The holiday was probably the best distraction.

As I step into the patisserie, the aroma of bread is divine. It's not a word I often use, but it's *so* good it is the only word that comes to mind. Buying freshly baked croissants in Paris almost causes the same amount of excitement as a Christmas market. There is truly something wonderful about strolling out in the early morning in Paris for baked goods. Why? I don't know, but it's wonderful, that's all I know. There is such an array of mouthwatering food it's dangerous, but I behave, only grabbing what I came for: croissants, before buying butter, jam, and fruit in the small supermarket next door.

I see Mum living it up Parisian-style in a cafe, eating a croissant and watching the world go by. I can't help but feel sad when I see her. She should be sitting with Dad right now, and I know she's missing him terribly as she sits there on her own. Paris was the first stop on their European trip just before he died, and I know grief, her ever-present companion, is making its presence known to her. When I wave to her, she brightens. I pop into the cafe and take a seat. We chat about Dad for a few minutes, and their time in Paris.

Wanting him here with us is a feeling that will never go away, but as we talk of what we might do today, we begin to smile again. We are in Paris, after all, and if distraction is required, then Paris is a good place for it.

The group splits for the morning as Anthony and the kids say they need to go shopping. They are acting mysterious, and I think they are shopping for my birthday present. Mum, Maree, David, and I visit the post office to buy boxes so we can send our excess crap home. And there is some crap, believe me. I buy two empty boxes from the post office, each ready to be filled with fourteen kilos of crap, but really we could have done with three. Between the seven of us, twenty-eight kilos of crap is sent home. Here's the word 'crap' again for good measure.

We hit lunchtime and visit my favourite local patisserie for the second time today. I'm no connoisseur of baguettes, but why is it that Paris has the yummiest baguettes in the world?

Crime against Hounds and Humanity

Without Anthony I've become the Mistress of the Maps, and I successfully direct us all towards the Pont Neuf Bridge to meet him and the kids at the Notre-Dame Cathedral. Located on an island in the Seine, Ile de la Cite, on which the Pont Neuf Bridge spans, the cathedral was on my to-do list prior to realising I would hit the church-wall on the trip. I still want to go though, as Notre-Dame has such an interesting history and the architecture is beautiful. On the last trip we were herded through so quickly on a city tour, we hardly got to see anything. Perhaps there will be a hunchback in wait this time. Who knows?

On the way I spot the cutest wirehaired dachshund puppy. I'm so excited the call comes out my mouth like a shriek, and I stumble over the word, which I've always said wrong anyway. I'm a lifelong dachshund owner but can't seem to get myself to call them 'dak-sunds.' I know it's a crime against hounds and humanity, but it always comes out as 'dash-hound,' but I can't help it. I've said it that way since I was three years old. It's way too late for me!

Before I know what I'm doing, I cross the street and ask for a pat. The lady smiles and picks him up for me to pat, and I'm so excited I can't breathe. Thoughts of a puppy friend for Charlie crowd my mind as I stroke his small head.

I am on two now! Sorry, Mum, (not sorry) you are last!

Dachshund Spotting Total:
Anthony 24, David, 4, Maree 3, Holly 3, Sam 3, Lisa 2, Mum 1

As soon as we meet Anthony and the kids at Notre-Dame, the kids can't wait to tell us Anthony has seen a dachshund. And guess what it was? A cute wirehaired puppy! When I show them the photo of *my* wirehaired dachshund puppy, Sam thinks there's a possibility Anthony's wirehaired sighting and mine are one and the same, even though we saw them an hour apart. Sam presses me to go onto Google maps to check the distance between the two sightings. He drills me with question after question.

Where were you when you saw it?
What did the owner look like?
What was the exact time you saw it?
Can a teeny tiny puppy walk that far in that time?
Could the owner have carried it for part of the way?

I don't care if it's the same dog; I'm having my dachshund spotting and formally approve the two separate sightings. It is the end of discussion, although Sam still wants to check Google maps when we have Wi-Fi to calculate the distance to puppy legs step ratio or something like that. I stopped listening.

Dachshund Spotting Total:
Anthony 25, David, 4, Maree 3, Holly 3, Sam 3, Lisa 2, Mum 1

You Say You Want a Revolution

Notre-Dame de Paris, French for 'Our Lady of Paris,' is such a beautiful church, and from what I've read, is a wonder of French Gothic architecture. The tour is interesting and free (running every day of the week in different languages), but rather than being about the architecture and history of the place, the visit ends up being more about religion, long talks on Bible stories and detailed descriptions of the Apostles all told with great fervor by our *very* enthusiastic and *very* religious American guide who says *many* times over in her broad accent, that the Notre-Dame is 'AWE [long pause] SOME.' And she is quite correct.

The facade of the cathedral is decorated with hundreds of statues and the grotesque shapes of gargoyles and chimera. There are statues of Adam and Eve, Virgin Mary and child, all the kings of Judah, the Apostles, and more.

It is thought that the foundation's stone was laid in 1163, followed by two centuries of construction. As always, these cathedrals lead me to think of Ken Follet's book *The Pillars of the Earth* and the lifetime of work masons dedicated to the building of a church. Nice work if you can get it!

The Hunchback of Notre Dame by Victor Hugo and the Disney movie are what placed the cathedral in the minds of many, including me. Perhaps we would have heard of it without the book and movie, but perhaps it wouldn't be here, as it is today, without the book. Victor Hugo, a champion of Gothic architecture, was dismayed at the time about how many Gothic structures were being destroyed, replaced, and rebuilt. It is said he initially wrote *Notre Dame de Paris* (*The Hunchback of Notre Dame*) to shine a light on the medieval architecture of Paris. The novel was a huge success in

France and led to the renovations we see here today. This excites me, the power words have. A book, a story, a fable, or a song can cause change, and to quote author Kathryn Heyman, 'Words can induce a revolution. A writer, a storyteller, can persuade an audience with their words.'

The interior of the Notre-Dame Cathedral is magnificent, and I fear that I'm unable to do it any justice with mere words.

Mother-and-Daughter Time

After waking this morning, I spend so long researching tours of the Normandy battlefields for our next stop that I forget Advent gifts. The sleepy-eyed children are sent back upstairs while I quickly come up with something. And then the idea comes to me like a bolt of lightening. I quickly organise it, call them back, and hand them a hastily scribbled clue of 'Just look around!' I video them capering about like monkeys until they find a Mars Bar chopped in half on saucers in the kitchen.

Their response: Pick up the game!

Today is a relaxed day with no particular plans, a free day devoted to whatever everyone wants to do. Maree and David shop and walk along the Seine together, Anthony goes for a run while the kids do what kids do best, flop around at the apartment and have some time to relax without me constantly telling them we are going somewhere. Mum and I wander the streets surrounding our apartment in Saint Germain before deciding a chocolate overload is required.

We take our seats in a French cafe with low lighting, tiny round tables, and to add to the experience, a good-looking French waiter. We order hot chocolate and a dessert plate with four miniature desserts of tiramisu, creme brulee, a macaron, and orange liqueur cake.

Mum is quiet and missing Dad, but happy. 'He's not here, but I'm so lucky to have this wonderful life and a family who loves me.' She looks out the window to the busy Paris street. 'And to be here on this trip.' She says this a lot, it's her pick-me-up if she is down about losing Dad. She has many older friends who don't have family support, so she feels fortunate. Many are in their 70s and 80s and on their own with no one to visit, let alone take them on a world trip. 'Sometimes I can't believe I'm actually here,' she comments with wonder.

'We wouldn't have it any other way,' I respond.

She's missing Karen, my sister, as well, as am I. It's been hard to keep in contact while travelling, an email and a phone call here and there, but by the time we see her and the rest of the family in New York City, we will have been away for nine weeks, so we'll be more than ready to see everyone. To put it in perspective, the level of excitement of our group becoming a party of twenty-six in New York City will be like 'seeing a Christmas market times infinity.' It's a tricky mathematical equation—look it up.

Mum and I talk of catching the metro over to Galleries Lafayette, the stunning department store on the Right Bank, but we want to go there with Maree and Holly as well, so we start to explore the Saint Germain area and find shops, a little Christmas market, and endless cafes and restaurants. It's a lovely area away from the hustle and bustle. We pop into Swarovski and buy Christmas gifts, and look through a shoe shop, but I resist buying anything that isn't essential (Swarovski teddy bear with a Santa hat aside) after sending fourteen kilos of crap home.

When I get back to the apartment, Sam and Holly are ready for their Paris Ferris wheel and ice-skating adventure. All have returned from their outings, and soon we set out to walk over to the Marche de Noel for some fun.

We line up for our tickets, and as we are in a queue and there is no escape from Holly, it is time for clapping and Concentration. The farther along the trip we go and the more places we see, then the game of Concentration becomes easier to play. We clap away calling out, one by one, all of the places we've seen so far on the trip. But as usual I trip up first, stuttering a response that doesn't sound remotely like the English language. Holly then turns on Maree and convinces her to play, and then Mum. But before long, we are ushered into two gondolas of the Ferris wheel, we four in one and the grandparents in another, to see the sights of Paris from above. Lucky for us it is a clear, cloud-free day and the views over the Seine, the Champs-Elysees to the Arc de Triomphe, and the Louvre are spectacular. Next up is lunch at the Marche de Noel and ice-skating. It's a lovely afternoon.

Flash Time

Tonight Anthony and I have a night to ourselves while the kids and grandparents have dinner at the 58 Tour Eiffel restaurant at the Eiffel Tower. Booked months ago as a gift from Mum, Anthony and I are going on a dinner cruise on the Seine. At $375 AUD per person, I am expecting the dinner to be a bit flash. The cheaper tickets meant sitting with other dinner guests on bigger tables, so I am guessing the 375 is mainly so Anthony and I have a table to ourselves. Ha! Mum knows Anthony so well. Making small talk with strangers while on a romantic dinner cruise is not his cup of tea.

The cruise is a most ridiculous splurge, but a big deal for Mum to send us on, so I am ready to enjoy.

I'm really looking forward to a night with Anthony but not nearly as excited about what I'm wearing. I slip on my only dress, a long-sleeved black dress with a flared skirt to the mid-calf. But when I put on my knee-high black boots, the ones I wear nearly every day that have a slight resemblance to gumboots, I'm not happy. Although Anthony thinks it looks fine, I feel ridiculous.

We have twenty minutes until we are being picked up by the tour company, so I dash out, singing out over my shoulder that I'm going out to buy stockings, which I do buy, but I have an ulterior motive. In a feat of shopping brilliance, I return fifteen minutes later with Geox high heels, and the fashion emergency is averted. But I failed at not buying non-essential items. I don't think anyone really expected me to succeed, did they?

The night begins at a dock beneath the towering light of the Eiffel Tower. I reach for the camera, and it's then I realise I'd forgotten it during the dress/gumboot dilemma. Anthony grabs my hand, and we board the Bateaux Parisiens' sightseeing boat. As we board, I assure Anthony we are sitting on our own after he sees the tables of four and eight on the boat. 'You'll only have me to talk to all night,' I assure him.

He does a teasing smile and looks at his watch, inquiring, 'How long is the cruise for?'

I laugh as we are taken through to the front of the boat to where there are only four two-person tables. We are seated right on the window with a glass-topped roof overhead, and within seconds our waiter is hovering with pink champagne and melt-in-your mouth cheese puffs.

'Isn't this nice?' I have to say. I know I say it a lot, but this *is* nice. I've been looking forward to a night out with my gorgeous man for weeks. Although at the moment, he is hiding under a holiday beard. Still gorgeous, but it's time to shave!

It is almost dark, and the lights of Paris start to glimmer as the boat glides along. We talk of our favourite parts of the holiday, the places we want to see more of, of Coco and Charlie and future holidays.

Soon we are brought foie gras duck confit with plum chutney and a veloute of shellfish, crayfish, and morel mushroom, and the accompanying white wine, followed by filet of beef tournedos with porcini mushrooms and leg of lamb with vegetables and poivrade sauce accompanied by a bottle of red wine, which is topped up constantly during the meal. Then there are aged cheeses and an array of little desserts with another glass of champagne.

We eat, talk, laugh, and watch the nightlights and sights of Paris slip by.

Holiday Uninterrupted

Here comes the hangover. It arrives with a force even a freshly baked French croissant can't budge. The kids are chucked a small chocolate each for Advent.

I drink loads of water, take paracetemol, and pretend like nothing's wrong. The holiday must go on, and I manage to navigate the Paris Metro with Mum, Holly, David, and Maree, scoff down McDonalds because that's what all hangovers require (or bacon and eggs), and admire the Christmas window displays and the magnificent Christmas tree nestled under the cupola inside the beautiful Galleries Lafayette department store. In its foggy state, my brain has a slight malfunction, and I almost buy a Diane Von Furstenberg signature wrap dress at 425 euros. I'm glad the sensible part of my brain woke up and made me put the dress back on the rack.

While we shop, Sam and Anthony hire bikes and ride around Paris for a few hours, up and down the banks of the Seine and through the park beneath the Eiffel Tower in wintery sunshine.

Chocolate Lessons

We all gather together along the Rue Royal for our afternoon activity which the kids chose months ago. Predicting they would be well and truly over city tours by now, I sent them to look on Viator.com and pick whatever they wanted for us all to do in Paris. The Paris Chocolate Tour was unanimously chosen by them both, and here we are—ready for some chocolate.

We meet the tour guide at Maxim's de Paris and have our first tasting before following the guide to Angelina's, a favourite cafe in Paris for tourists where Coco Chanel once visited for her chocolate fix. Here we bypass the long queue for our chocolate tasting. We also drink hot chocolate so rich it's almost like drinking melted chocolate.

Afterwards we pop into Pierre Herme, Les Marquis, and Jean Paul Hevin's Chocolatier for more tastings. We taste chocolate, truffles, and macarons, and drool over trays and trays of some of the most delectable-looking desserts I've ever seen. While walking we hear historical facts about Paris and the first arrondissement, as well as the history of chocolate. Most of the shops we visit have been operating for over a hundred years. Some are fairly new but are making a name for themselves in the world of chocolate, competing well with the older chocolate houses.

And even though my hangover from hell persists and there are times when I want to simply lie down on the footpath and die, I really like the tour. Seriously, it is one of those hangovers where simply walking and talking is a supreme effort. Deep breaths, sips of water, and chocolate get me through.

After the tour Anthony spots another dachshund in the distance, although it cannot be confirmed until it comes closer. There is much excitement when we see it's a brown, longhaired puppy. It seems that Paris is the place of dachshund puppies, and the call is formally confirmed even though Anthony with his bionic eyesight advises he didn't need the official confirmation. That's it, I know who he is now. He is the Bionic Man.

Maree somehow misses the entire dachshund spotting *and* discussion, and as the puppy passes us, she yells out her own dachshund call. Too late, Maree, way too late. Your son was on to that five minutes ago. You had no chance!

Dachshund Spotting Total:
Anthony 26, David, 4, Maree 3, Holly 3, Sam 3, Lisa 2, Mum 1

Not So Bionic Now!

It's now 4:30 pm, and we're all pretty tired, especially me since, you know . . . I'm dying here. We've been walking since 10 am, the tour finished at 4:30, and we still have a half an hour walk back to our apartment. For the first time, the Master of the Maps, Anthony, is lost. I am secretly a little bit happy, and despite the hangover, I am enjoying our lostness. We've gotten ourselves into a little maze of streets somewhere near the Louvre. We can see the museum building and know it is on the bank of the Seine, but do you think we can get there? No.

After some time, we send Mum, Maree, and David back in a cab. It doesn't take Anthony and me long to work it out though, and within twenty minutes of sending the oldies back, we're back at our apartment for a dinner of takeaway pizza and packing up for the next stop on our trip: Bayeux.

(18)

BAYEUX, FRANCE

Date: *December 8*
Location: *Paris – Bayeux*
Nights: *3*
Dachshunds so far: *42*

Quiet Time

Bayeux is a small town on the Normandy Coast, famous for the Bayeux Tapestry and the site of the infamous D-Day invasion of Nazi-occupied France on June 6, 1944. This is the reason we are visiting, but I'm also looking forward to a few quiet days. We have one entire day, my birthday on the ninth of December, with no tourist activities organised although I'm sure we'll find something to fill it with!

We arrive at our festive accommodation, the Hotel Reine Mathilde, and settle into our rooms in a separate building across a little bridge and canal. We unpack bags, set up the Advent calendar and wooden Christmas tree, and all go for a walk around the quiet town. Many of the shops are closed for the winter or only open limited hours, and we don't see many people about. But I don't care; it's nice that it's so quiet after so many busy cities.

We almost finish a loop around the whole town when Anthony makes a loud dachshund call. It is hotly contested between the group, as the dog is *so* far away; to me it could be any breed of small dog. 'No, it's not,' I argue, but Anthony is confident it is.

Then David adds, 'No, it's not a dachshund shape.'

But Anthony only smiles, saying, 'You'll see.'

Sam and Holly dash ahead on the pathway to investigate, running as fast as they can. It's the first time I've seen Holly run in weeks. After a couple of minutes, they run back, yelling and smiling.

'It *is* a dachshund!' Holly yells.

Sam adds, 'A wirehaired one!'

Eventually an older gentleman and a dachshund pass us. I take a photo of this elusive creature only Anthony seems to be able to spot. Maree makes a desperate dachshund call when she sees it, but again, way too late.

Dachshund Spotting Total:
Anthony 27, David 4, Maree 3, Holly 3, Sam 3, Lisa 2, Mum 1

The little restaurant in our hotel is warm and festive with Christmas decorations and friendly staff, so we don't even try to look for somewhere to go for dinner. We enjoy pizza, burgers, crepes, French chicken casserole, and fettuccini carbonara. It is all really nice, and the service is fantastic. We feel at home in the quiet hotel.

Sexy Back

Today is my birthday, and it's time for presents. Anthony and kids managed to find a black and red purse with a dachshund on it. I try to claim it as a dachshund spotting, but no luck there, even on my birthday. I'm also given a red beanie, (a non-scratchy one, of course—no one wants to hear me whining), a beautiful snowflake charm from Mum, and a delicate dragonfly pendant from David and Maree. Thank you, family!

We all set out for a walk to explore the town together. Bayeux is quite a pretty town with meandering canals, little bridges, and old mill wheels turning in the waters of the canals.

Holly and Sam spot a dachshund across a canal, and their simultaneous cry of 'Dachshund!' rings loud in the quiet. There is some heated sibling chat about who saw it first, but the call is deemed a tie, and half a point each is awarded. A discussion follows about who has the 'head end' of the dog and who has the 'bum end.' Both want the head. Who would want the poo end anyway? Talk then turns to a catdog (a cartoon the kids used to watch) style of dachshund with two heads or two bums.

Dachshund Spotting Total:
Anthony 27, David 4, Holly 3.5, Sam 3.5, Maree 3, Lisa 2, Mum 1

The church spire of the Notre-Dame Cathedral of Bayeux rises from between two narrow streets, and I snap a photo. As much as I am not very religious, there is something about the tall spire and the history and architecture of churches that draws me in, especially the understated ones with stone interiors and without all the gaudy decoration. It's hushed inside, and a service is taking place, so we stand quietly at the back and gaze around. Built in the eleventh century in the time of William the Conqueror, the cathedral was where the Duke of Normandy forced Harold, Earl of Wessex, to take oath, so it packs a historical punch within the walls. After a few minutes we slip back out into the cold.

Even though it is a day of no tourist activities, you can't pay a visit to Bayeux without feasting your eyes upon the seventy-metre long Bayeux Tapestry at La Tapisserie De Bayeux. Who doesn't want to see that?

Created nine hundred years ago and telling the embroidered story of the historic events of William, Duke of Normandy's conquest of England, it is definitely an interesting relic to see. In fifty vivid, detailed scenes, the tapestry reveals the lead up to and the Battle of Hastings on October 14, 1066.

If you want to know all about the battle, go no farther than watching this wonderful video clip on YouTube (https://www.youtube.com/watch?v=bQ8A5gRe_Dw) describing the Bayeux tapestry to the tune of Justin Timberlake's song, 'Sexy Back.' You'll never sing it with Justin's lines again! Ah, the amount of times we have watched this in hysterics is ridiculous. I must share it, so everyone can have this inventive song stuck in his or her heads as well. I'm nice like that. Sew it, girl!

For lunch we grab baguettes and head back to the hotel for a nap. While on the bed, the kids catch Anthony and I out, and no, it's not what you think. We are caught looking for a dachshund puppy on the Internet, and they are so excited. Holly has tears in her eyes as she talks of Charlie having a friend to play with. We all want that—we keep looking at the video of Charlie playing with our house sitter's German shepherd, Merlot, and we know he needs a friend. He is quite the lazy dog, and without another dog to play with, I suspect he will become even lazier.

It feels like a betrayal looking online for puppies when Coco has only been gone not much longer than the length of our trip. And it still doesn't seem real that she is gone. So searching for puppies is exciting but doesn't quite feel right at the same time. After going onto three or four dachshund websites in the Sydney area, there are no pups available. Putting the computer away, I suggest a game of cards. I don't want to get the kids' hopes up with puppies; sometimes it takes months to find a pup from a registered breeder.

We all dress for dinner and go wandering around the town, looking for restaurants, but none are open. We finally find one with activity inside, but upon checking, we are told it doesn't open for another hour. For weary travellers a restaurant opening at 7 pm is too late. Is that pathetic? Yes, probably, but it's bitterly cold, we have a big tour tomorrow, and Anthony has a 4 am work phone call, so the earlier to bed the better.

We go back to our favourite Bayeux restaurant in the Hotel Reine Mathilde. The staff are so lovely, the restaurant charming, and the food awesome. I'm with my beautiful family on my birthday, and somehow, in this quiet town, Anthony has managed to find a fabulous cake, which the restaurant serves up with toffee shards and chocolate shavings. Feeling fortunate.

Forever Heroes

After breakfast Stuart Robertson of Normandy Battlefield Tours picks us up for a tour of the D-Day battlegrounds, beaches, and cemeteries. He is passionate about the details of the battles and he sweeps us along with his stories and descriptions, including recounts from the many veterans he's met over the years.

Much is known of the Normandy landings on June 6, 1944, and like many war stories, what happened here has become legendary. The people who landed upon these shores will forever be heroes. The Allied invasion of Normandy during World War Two to liberate Northwestern Europe from Nazi occupation, as Stuart describes, was 'the largest amphibious invasion the world had ever seen.'

We start the tour at Omaha Beach where some of the bloodiest battles took place. There were simultaneous landings of thousands of British, American, and Canadian troops along five beaches of the Normandy Coast. The landing on this strip of sand is the stuff of legend and inspired the twenty-seven-minute scene at the beginning of *Saving Private Ryan*. With the firepower of four hundred bullets per second directed towards them from the German army, thousands of landmines beneath their feet, and millions of obstacles littering the beach, the Allied soldiers' mission was to take the beach and ultimately liberate France.

Stuart says Hollywood did an accurate job of what happened here that day. It's not hard to picture that scene in *Saving Private Ryan*. It is gut-wrenching, bloody, confusing, and hammering with the noise of bullets, explosions, and the anguished screams of dying men.

We hear of the airborne bombardment days before the amphibious landing. Of how hundreds of planes dropped thousands of bombs, destroying bridges across the Loire and Seine rivers to isolate the Germans and disrupt their efforts to stop the invasion. The Germans knew it was coming, how could they not with the Allies' obvious preparations off the coast of Normandy? All they could do was try to stop it.

We then continue on to the American cemetery. It is the second largest American cemetery after Arlington in Washington, DC. The grounds are beautiful, and we walk amongst memorials, and past thousands of white crosses, stark against the lush green of the lawns.

Afterwards Stuart takes us to the German cemetery. Although neat and tidy and park-like, it is not white and pristine like the American cemetery and looks older and more ancient then it actually is. The gravestones are rock, affected by time, weather, and moss, and rest heavy in the green grass. Hitler spread his armies wide, fighting a losing battle on too many fronts, and suffered massive losses in his campaign in the Soviet Union. Towards the end of the war, Stuart tells us, many in the German army at Normandy were foreign conscripts from Poland, Latvia, Lithuania, Estonia, Ukraine, and more, and that many were forced to play a part in the war.

We continue to Arromanches where the yearly veterans' march takes place. It is here, at Arromanches, that the Allied forces built a man-made harbour to keep ammunition and supplies to the troops, which, for the times, was an engineering masterpiece. The artificial harbour was (in part) built with sunken ships and huge concrete blocks towed across the channel, contributing to the four miles of breakwater, some of which are still visible from the beach. Stuart tells us that with each storm that hits the coast, they are disappearing.

The harbour, or man-made port, had floating platforms, roadways, piers, pontoons, and bridges. Tanks, jeeps, ammunition, supplies, and thousands of soldiers were brought from England without having to approach the Nazi-occupied coast of France. How they completed this harbour was amazing. Thousands of ships and landing craft delivered nearly two hundred thousand vehicles and six hundred thousand tonnes of supplies in the first three weeks of the operation. Incredible.

We walk along the shore while the kids race around below on the beach at Arromanches, cartwheeling and playing chase. Out in the water, I can see what remains of the artificial harbour. The concrete blocks rest in the water like sentinels, guarding the harbour and reminding future generations of what played out here in 1944.

At Juno Beach, where the Canadian forces landed, Stuart recounts a personal story of a Canadian veteran and his experience when he landed on the beach. It is a story of death, losing mates, and survival. We walk along the quiet coast and rocky beach past white swimming huts, closed up tight for the winter, to the Canadian Museum where we learn more of Canada's involvement in the war and D-Day.

Just as we leave Juno Beach, Holly spots a dachshund. She makes the call, but there is some debate. Eventually Anthony and I decide it's a standard (the larger breed of dachshund), wirehaired dachshund. Sam is one hundred percent sure it's not a dachshund and claims it's a Scottish terrier, as the wirehaired dachshunds have a scruffy face that gives the appearance of a terrier. But the undeniable long nose is present, the long body, and the cheeky disposition. The point is awarded. Sam's not happy as Holly is now ahead of him.

Dachshund Spotting Total:
Anthony 27, David 4, Holly 4.5, Sam 3.5, Maree 3, Lisa 2, Mum 1

Stop for a sec—do you hear that ringing?
London is calling!

(19)

LONDON, ENGLAND

Date: December 11
Location: Bayeux – London
Nights: 4
Dachshunds so far: 45

Music to My Ears

We arrive by Eurostar to London's busy Saint Pancras Station and haul our bags from the train and through the busy station. I've loved our travel so far, but after eight weeks, it certainly feels nice to understand what people are saying again! We've had no particular issues with language on the trip, except perhaps in Russia, but still, hearing the sound of words I can understand is comforting.

We jump in two cabs, the oldies going one way and Anthony, the kids, and I going another. There are obviously many different ways to Northumberland Avenue, and we arrive ten minutes after the others with a larger cab fare. We check into what are great apartments at the Citadines Trafalgar Square, and, oh joy, there are washing machines!

As soon as we unpack, we're out the door into the cold of wintery London. We head straight towards the light and sounds of Trafalgar Square. It's only our second time to London, but like Paris, I don't think I can ever tire of it. I have to admit both of my visits have been at Christmas, and there is a definite festive vibe with the brightly lit Christmas decorations on shopfronts, streetlights, and buildings, adding to the atmosphere of an already vibrant city.

We walk along the Strand, passing by red double-decker buses, a vintage style Burberry van, and the busy ice rink at Somerset House, before ducking down a narrow street to the banks of the Thames. Ahead, the iconic riverside vista of London reflects in the dark waters of the river and looks pretty grand. The London Eye dominates, twinkling on its slow revolution, looming high above the usual sites of Big Ben and the Houses of Parliament.

But what catches my eye are the multi-coloured lights, Christmas decorations, and the telltale chalets of a Christmas market situated between the London Eye and Waterloo Bridge. I may have already Googled the Southbank Centre Christmas Markets, and I may have already known they were within walking distance from our apartments. When I pause in my walking and listen carefully, I hear them calling—*Lisa . . . come and buy stuff, we have mulled wine, sausages, hog roasts, sugar-covered things, roasted nuts, rides, decorations and . . . stuff. Come to me, my child, and buy, buy, buy!*

There is no time to visit right now though, as all are hungry and Anthony is craving a meat pie, his favourite of all British food, followed closely by bangers and mash. We're almost back at the hotel and don't fancy a big search for meat pie, but luckily, the

Sherlock Holmes Pub is not far up the road from the hotel. Plus, it is complete with a museum area dedicated to the famous sleuth.

We make our way upstairs to the dining room and delight over the menu as if we haven't eaten in months. Even after the great food we've been eating, the sight of this familiar-looking fare is exciting. Bring us meat pies, Yorkshire puddings, mushy peas, fish and chips, and toads in holes, and don't forget the gravy! A selection of meals is ordered, from Mrs. Hudson's steak and ale pie, Dr. Watson's traditional Sunday lunch, the Hounds of Baskerville toad in the hole, and the Retired Colourman's fish and chips.

The usual excited grin settles on my face as we cross the Waterloo Bridge after dinner to visit the Christmas markets. It's freezing, and all have shoulders hunched against the cold. I'm still hoping for snow but of course, not too much, just a sprinkling—I don't need any airport closures mucking up my plans. However, the weather websites are not my friends as there is no sign, whatsoever, of snow on the horizon.

Holly and I spy a carousel with big-people horses, and after the giggle-fest in Strasbourg when we went on a mini carousal for small children, we decide we must come back another time for a ride.

Mum is staying in the two-bedroom apartment with us, and it's so nice to stay together. We haven't done this in a while, with mostly separate hotel rooms along the way. And it's lovely to have a cup of tea before bed and a chat. She is in with Holly, and the two snuggle together in bed. Night all!

A Magic-Filled Day and Evening

The first activity on the schedule is the Harry Potter studio tour (for me, Anthony, and the kids anyway). Mum, Maree, and David head off for a day cruising the Thames, stopping for coffee and cake, and touring around on the hop-on, hop-off bus to see the sights of London.

We make our way to Euston Station and then onto Watford Junction, about thirty minutes from London and not far from the Warner Brothers Studio. Holly is *so* excited it's not funny. There are smiles aplenty from my girl the whole way out to Watford, and just quietly, I'm pretty excited as well! As a reader and writer of fantasy fiction, this is right up my Diagon Alley.

At Watford Junction we hop on a special Harry Potter double-decker bus to the studios. Soon after arrival we're ushered together with a group of visitors into a room for a welcome and a gee-up from a wizardy character, before we're led towards the arched timber doors of the Great Hall, the one used in the movies! After a suitable excitement-filled build-up, the doors sweep open, and there is a rumble of *oohs* and *aahs* from the gathered group, including Holly. The hall is decorated for a Hogwarts Christmas with Christmas trees, crackers, garlands, wreaths, and huge Christmas puddings. It's shimmery and warm and magical, and I have to say it's pretty cool to see this set!

Onwards we go through the fantastical imagination of JK Rowling. We see wizards' wands, outfits and hats, cauldrons, the Gryffindor dorm room, potions, and the Mirror of Erised. Holly poses before the snaky round door to the Chamber of Secrets and Dumbledore's office. We check out potions, horcruxes, Hagrid's hut, and a hippogriff. There are monsters, spiders, dragons, and a full-scale model of Hogwarts, which is incredible. Wandering along Diagon Alley, we peer through the window of Ollivanders: Makers of Fine Wands and Weasley's Joke Shop and all the rest.

Anthony is enjoying it too, a lot more than he thought. Even though he hasn't read the books or seen the movies, he's fascinated with what goes on behind the scenes. He learns that Voldemort killed Harry's parents and thought he'd better let Holly know in case she didn't know.

The scale of the sets, the thousands of props, the technical drawings, models built, and hundreds of processes bringing these movies to life on screen are amazing. The four of us take a ride in the car Ron stole, and Holly rides a broomstick over Hogwarts (both on the green screen). Use your imagination, people!

After a couple of hours, we finally make our way through to Privet Drive and the Knight Bus, and order a few cups of butter beer. Do we like it? Hmm, we're not convinced about butter beer. But not to matter, even if we don't like it, there is still the gift shop to visit, which is quite possibly the best gift shop in the entire world. We ride the bus and train back to London, eating chocolate frogs and trying to avoid eating snot, dirt, and earwax Bertie Bott's Every Flavour Beans.

In London, Holly and I leave the boys for some girl time, which means shopping, eating, and visiting Harrods, the iconic luxury department store. We wander through the Harrods gift shop, the second best gift shop after Harry Potter, buy Christmas presents, check out the toy department and the Harrods pet section, which includes a four-poster dog bed worth £1,600 and another with dachshunds on it, both of which Holly suggests we buy, and I say no. What restraint I showed! We walk along the busy Piccadilly

Circus and talk of all the properties on the Monopoly Board we've been to.

After a full day of Hogwarts and Harrods for us, Thames River cruises and the hop-on, hop-off buses for the oldies, for the evening we dress to see *The Nutcracker* performed by the English National Ballet at the Coliseum Theatre. The theatre is beautiful, the Christmas Eve story of Clara and her nutcracker is magical, and the dancers are incredible.

Even though the boys weren't overly excited to go, Sam does say, 'It wasn't that bad,' but then adds, 'It wasn't great, though. My favourite part was the end.'

Anthony says he enjoyed it as well, and I know he likes to experience new things while we're travelling, but his face is screwed up in a way that I think what he really wants to say is, 'I'd rather be having a pint at the pub.' David decides the ballet was not for him and thinks a quiet night in the apartment is infinitely more interesting. But the most important people, the ladies, were mesmerised. Nice way to spend the evening in London!

Stuff, Stuff, Stuff, Stuff, Stuff, Stuff, Stuff, Stuff & More Stuff!

After tricky Christmas riddles and chocolate coins for Advent, Holly doesn't comprehend the word 'share' and with a strange smile clutches the gold coins to her chest like Gollum with the One Ring to rule them all.

Anthony, Maree, David, and Sam do a tour of Lord's Cricket Ground. Sam, who is not a fan of cricket but thought a visit to say he had been there would be worth it, declared the tour better than the ballet.

Anthony, Maree, and David really enjoyed the tour, and after hearing Anthony talk about some of things they saw and interesting facts about the ground and history of the Ashes, I realised it is a big part of Australian and British sporting history and that maybe I should have gone too, but . . . Holly and I have shopping to do! And Mum put aside the day to go to Harrods and look at a few more things on the hop-on, hop-off bus.

Holly and I start to make our way up to the Strand, get a little turned around, and find ourselves wandering along narrow, festive streets decorated with Christmas decorations. We end up in Covent Garden quite by accident, and I snap a photo of Holly under the big Christmas tree towering in the square. We look at Lego masterpieces and walk through the beautifully decorated Apple Market, an artist marketplace. Huge Christmas baubles hang from the ceiling, giant-sized red-striped candy canes hang over our heads, and sparkling garlands drape from shop to shop.

We buy a few Christmas presents, a sketch of London, and listen to a tremendous classical quartet playing Christmas carols on a lower level. We lean out over the balcony to watch and listen for a while before looking through an art gallery with some nice dachshund art. Did we buy any? Of course! Somewhere along the way I seem to have forgotten to stop buying stuff. How could we resist this though?

Holly and I walk hand in hand back to the hotel, dump our shopping bags, and continue to the Christmas market on Southbank for our ride on the carousel. Thankfully, this one is large enough for us, and we climb onto Savanah and Cathy, our mounts for the ride, and enjoy a spinny, giggly twirl.

I, of course, buy more crap at the market, even though we had recently cleared our bags of crap when sending things home in Paris. This crap purchase is in the form of hand warmers for pockets, little gel pouches that supposedly keep cold fingers warm. I buy two for everyone since everyone has two hands. I spend way too many pounds on the stupidest thing ever as they do not merely need resting in boiling water to heat as the lady told me, they need to be consistently boiled for several minutes, which we have *no* way of doing. So, not only do we have no way to heat them, they are heavy, and there have been *so* been many discussions in the last few days about our twenty-one-kilo weight limit for our flight to Dublin and the subsequent de-cluttering bags of all unnecessary items that it should have stopped me from buying extra crap. But no.

This will be our first flight since flying from Turkey to Moscow, and we haven't had to think about bag weights for weeks. So what do *I* do? Buy heavy, useless crap for way too much money. The hand warmers are promptly binned, all fourteen of them. Purchase fail and brain malfunction by me. Oh dear.

I cheer up after my stupidity as we dress for our fancy dinner at Gordon Ramsey's restaurant, the Savoy Grill in the Savoy Hotel with just the four of us. I am pleased to say that my high heels, bought so swiftly in Paris, get another wear. It is an absolutely beautiful meal with impeccable service and a fabulous treat to do with the kids. They look so grown up!

Mum, Maree, and David return to the old favourite, the Sherlock Holmes Pub, for dinner, as the ladies were craving Eton mess, a mix of meringue, whipped cream, and strawberries. Although they all enjoyed fish and chips, roast pork, and Yorkshire pudding, it isn't until after eating their main meal that they are told there is no

Eton mess. They settle for apple pie and ice cream as someone must have stolen all the Eton mess and Sherlock Holmes and Watson couldn't find it. Nice detectives they are.

Football Fun

The first half of today is filled with walks along Piccadilly Circus, Regent Street, and Oxford Street, before I wander off on my own to go past Buckingham Palace, Saint James Park, Big Ben, and along the Thames back to the hotel.

Then it's time for the Chelsea v. Crystal Palace football game at Stamford Bridge. Anthony, the kids, David, and I jump into a London cab and head out to the game while Mum and Maree do a London City tour to the White Tower and Saint Paul's Cathedral.

Anthony sees a dachshund from the cab from the other side of the car through Sam's window. Sam blames me for a lost sighting as I distracted him a nanosecond before to show him my freakishly long pinky nail, which is described by Anthony as a witch's nail.

From here on in I will forever be blamed for distracting Sam at the precise moment a dachshund came into view with my witch's nail. I will never, *ever* be forgiven, as not only was it a really cute dachshund, but Sam was specifically keeping an eye out as it would have made him even with Holly again in the competition. So basically I failed him as a mother.

Dachshund Spotting Total:
Anthony 28, David 4, Holly 4.5, Sam 3.5, Maree 3, Lisa 2, Mum 1

I never thought we would see this many dachshunds. They are well-liked dogs, I know that, but when I grew up, dachshunds were not often seen in Australia. I don't remember seeing many dachshunds when out and about as a child. But when *we* were out with ours, people would go crazy over them.

We take our seats to watch the football, and as the stadium fills, the chanting and singing begins, mainly from the Crystal Palace fans. It's interesting to see that the Crystal Palace fans are seated in one area with security guards lining the border the whole way around. You don't see that in Australia. We watch the warm-up and gee-up from the Chelsea mascot and Santa, and settle in to watch the match. The game is great, and although I'm not a huge sporting fan, soccer is something I don't mind, having watched Sam play for the last ten years. Chelsea wins 2–1!

It takes us a while to get home with all the crowds, but after a *big* walk to Sloane Square, we manage to grab a cab back to Trafalgar Square. The taxi drops us off short of the hotel, as there is so much traffic, but not only vehicles! As we walk down Northumberland Avenue, there are hundreds of people in Santa suits on skates and rollerblades singing Christmas carols. We stand and watch the whole procession go buy.

The people in London are well-dressed for Christmas, and apart from the Santas on skates, in the few days we've been here, I've lost count of how many people I've seen in knitted reindeer jumpers, Santa jumpers, Santa hats, and Santa suits. I love it! Holly and I decide it is time for us to wear Santa hats instead of beanies.

I catch up with Mum and Maree for a cup of tea before bed and hear all about their day visiting Saint Paul's Cathedral, the Tower of London, and a river cruise along the Thames.

Tomorrow we depart for Dublin where both the children will be keeping a close eye out for a leprechaun riding a dachshund—it's their only chance to beat Anthony in the dachshund-spotting competition. I believe in magic. It might well happen.

(20)

DUBLIN, IRELAND

Date: December 15
Location: London – Dublin
Nights: 4
Dachshunds so far: 46

Mystical Ireland

No matter how much fiddling has gone on with the luggage, we still have trouble at the airport checking in, and things must be moved and shuffled around bags. Yes, we're the family in front of the check-in desk trying to redistribute weight.

We arrive on our bumpy Aer Lingus flight to Dublin before waiting for a long, frustrating hour for our so-called transfer, which ends up being an old, dirty taxi. We could have caught a taxi an hour earlier ourselves. We could have walked *all* the way to Dublin with our suitcases dragging behind us. *Hint:* Don't book an airport transfer in Dublin—catch a taxi. But anyway, the taxi driver is a wonderfully friendly Irishman with a leprechaun (not riding a dachshund) dangling from his rearview mirror. It doesn't appear to be his fault, so we have no problem with him.

Our rooms aren't ready at what is one of our few splurge hotels on the trip, the Westin in Dublin. The hotel is pretty nice, as is its location, but there is no time to hang around as the long wait at the airport means a quick lunch before meeting Colette, our guide, to show us around the sights of Dublin. The kids are hoping for some dachshund sightings, and after so long joking about spotting a leprechaun riding a dachshund, they are keeping their eyes peeled. 'You never know,' I tell the kids, 'We're in Ireland, it's pretty mystical. Anything could happen!'

History Lessons with Colette

It's *so* cold and drizzly today that the thought of taking my gloves off to take notes on my phone while on the walking tour is not appealing. Hoods are up around cold faces as we follow Colette down O'Connell Street, over the River Liffey, and down one of the main streets of Dublin.

We pause before the statue of Daniel O'Connell, a famous political leader and reformist who amongst many things, campaigned for Catholic emancipation that (in short) would give Irish Catholics the right to become members of parliament. As we stand before the General Post Office, which housed the provisional government during the Irish rebellion in 1916, Colette tells us of Ireland's troubled past, unrest, rebellion, fighting, and famines, and its rough beginnings to becoming an independent nation.

We are taken up Henry Street and pop into a bar that was once a church where the famous brewer Guinness was married. Not long after, we gaze up to the spires of Christ Church Cathedral, a church founded in 1050 that houses the mummified remains of a mouse and a cat in the crypt.

We stand before a memorial to Veronica Guerin, stroll through Dublin Castle, learn of Dublin's early Viking beginnings in the twelfth century, and walk through the many cobblestone streets of Dublin's cultural hub, Temple Bar, the pub and restaurant district.

Next up are the grounds of Trinity College, Dublin's famous university founded in 1592 by Queen Elizabeth I. Visiting the Trinity College Old Library has been something I've been looking forward to the entire trip, but I soon find out that the walking tour does not include it. Lucky we have a full free day while we are here. Trinity College Old Library, you are formally slotted into the free day.

We keep a look out for long-bodied hounds, but none are seen, and neither is a leprechaun.

Even though all of us are fairly tired and could do with a night in, we rouse ourselves and brave the bitter cold to go to dinner in Temple Bar. We come across O'Neill's Pub, an Irish bar at its best with nooks and crannies, tables nestled within, live music, plenty of ale, and the Irish! Decorated with Christmas cheer, garlands, holly, and twinkling lights, it's warm and friendly. We decide the carvery menu is for us and have our plates filled with a meal that makes me feel right at home: roast meat, vegetables, Yorkshire puddings and gravy, and corned beef and cabbage.

A Filthy Kiss

Anthony, the kids, Mum, and I have an early start for our twelve-hour tour to Cork and Blarney Castle. Maree and David have been to Blarney Castle before so stay in Dublin for the day. We brave the early morning cold to meet the bus at 6:40 am with our breakfast bags provided by the Westin.

After a three-hour drive and perhaps a nap or two, we arrive to Blarney Castle, the six hundred-year-old ruins built by Cormac MacCarthy and home to the famous Blarney Stone. We hop off the bus with warnings from the driver, strict instructions of the return and time, plus the comment, 'It's a long way back to Dublin (should you not be back to the bus in time).'

We set off through the lush green grounds surrounding the castle, walking along a pathway over streams, rolling green lawns, and gardens, until we reach the castle. It rises up high above on an eight-metre rocky base, the window slits narrow for arrows to be rained upon ancient enemies. We wind around and up a slope to the entrance, and I snap a photo of Sam performing more community service, helping Grandma up the hill. We enter through a narrow set of uneven, roughly hewn steps, past walls with moss collecting in the nooks and crannies of the ancient stones.

Shafts of light stream through the narrow arrow slits in the castle walls with the picturesque streams and greenery of the gardens outside framed like a piece of art. A little red-breasted robin hops about on the rocky sill before taking flight when Sam pokes his face in front of my camera as I try to take a photo. He grins and continues to pose in nearly every photo, taking on what seems to be the self-imposed title of court jester.

Eventually, we wind our way up to the top to see the famous Blarney Stone while Mum waits below, as the steps are too uneven for her. She waves from below, and I take a photo of her smiling face.

There are many legends about the tradition of kissing the Blarney Stone, from blessings from the goddess Clíodhna, to it being a portion of the great rocks of Stonehenge or part of the Stone of Scone and gifted to Cormac McCarthy from Robert the Bruce. Who knows, but it certainly makes for a great tourist attraction! Kissing the Blarney Stone will, according to myth and legend, give the kisser the gift of gab from eloquence to flattery.

Holly is the only one willing to kiss the stone. She lies on her back, arches backwards, and holds onto metal poles while the attendant holds her. 'Good luck, Holly!' Mum calls from below. Holly kisses what is possibly a germ-ridden rock and comes back up smiling! Well done! Has the gift of the gab been received? Only time will tell.

We go to leave, only to be told the stairways are one way, so Mum must make her way up to the top, bad knee and all, with the help of Holly and Sam pushing her from behind. To come down the stairs, she goes down backwards and eventually makes it out.

On our stroll back through the gardens to the bus, we pass by the grand old mansion of Blarney House, follow timbered pathways past waterfalls, moss-covered rocks, and over-hanging trees. Seemingly mad today, perhaps released from cities and walking tours, the children caper about, racing and chasing each other. Anthony wanders ahead, hands behind his back, contemplating not yelling at the kids, perhaps. Ha! I remark to Mum that perhaps the trip, so far, has not included enough play or parks, but it's nearly over now. In two days time we'll meet our close friends and their kids, and then only days after there will be thirteen children gathered in New York City.

We return to the bus and wait and wait. Ten minutes after the time imposed by the driver, two groups return to the bus full of fake, laughing apologies. 'Oh, we weren't watching the time!' one of them cries. The bus driver is not happy. Neither is Anthony. So rude!

From 0 to 9

My Advent ideas are seriously lacking. Next year I am going to start preparing scavenger hunts, riddles, and activities early in the year.

Today the kids are told, 'Look somewhere Christmassy! Go!' There is some confusion and turning in circles before they both realise there are only two Christmassy things in the room—the Advent Calendar and the little wooden Christmas tree. It doesn't take them long to find little Kinder chocolates in the little pockets nestled in Santa's big beard on the Advent calendar. The mind-twisting riddles continue with 'Ask Dad for a clue,' with the prize being a hug. What?

'Where's the chocolate?' they want to know.

I confound them with the next clue, 'Look where Dad might do some work,' which they cannot work out. My video of them searching the room is watched over and over again by the laughing children who cannot fathom where someone might do work in a hotel room. At the desk, perhaps? Oh, yeah. Win for Mum.

Holly and I have been desperate, *desperate* I tell ya, for Santa hats, so that's what we set out to do while Anthony and David visit the Guinness Brewery, Mum and Maree wander through the Grafton Street shops, and Sam hangs out at the hotel.

Holly and I head out, but not to the Grafton Street shopping strip, but down O'Connell Street to a long mall and JC Penny, a department store that Holly is eager to look in. Along the way Santa hats and Santa sacks are bought in the markets in the mall, and we immediately swap beanies for red and white hats and join the Christmas festivities.

In JC Penney we come across full-sized fleece Santa suit onesies. They are big, cumbersome, and won't fit in our suitcases—and we want them! We stay in the shop for way too long while I resist buying the four onesies. 'It's a bad idea,' I tell Holly, 'our suitcases are full. Each onesie is the size of a rolled-up sleeping bag!' I'm still recovering from my gel hand warmer purchase in London and don't want another veil of stupidity to shroud my decision-making.

We walk away, onesie-less and sad. 'I'll talk to Dad and see what he thinks,' I say to Holly. To her that means no. I know we have a thirty-two-kilo limit when we fly to the USA, but we also have several internal flights over there in which our luggage limit will be back to twenty-two kilos. And there is also a question of space.

When we get to the hotel, I hesitantly pitch the crazy idea of buying four bulky Santa suit onesies to Anthony. I am expecting Anthony's usual little smile when I present a crazy suggestion, but he grins! Not only does he want to get them, right now, he also wants to buy nine! NINE! Adding five more onesies for our friends, Heidi and Anthony and their children whom we're meeting in Boston in a few days.

'I'll make them fit,' he asserts confidently.

Mum laughs and thinks we are absolutely mad, but the four of us head back out, purchase nine Santa suit onesies, return to the hotel with our bulky shopping bags and get our Santa on! Plenty of laughter follows as we race along the hotel hallway to show Maree and David our new purchases. Anthony lounges in his Santa suit onesie catching up on work.

Although there is talk of wearing our new outfits for the afternoon visit to the Trinity College Old Library and the Book of Kells, Holly and I settle on just wearing our Santa hats.

Old Library Wonder

The Old Library is the largest library in Ireland. And, not only is it one of the most notable libraries in the world, it is home to the Book of Kells, a ninth century, illuminated manuscript that I'm excited to see.

I step into the main chamber of the Old Library, called the Long Room for its length of sixty-five metres, and all I can think is—wow. It takes my breath away. Built in the early 1700s, it is a glorious room with a lofty arched ceiling, marble busts, winding spiral staircases, and dark timber bookcases housing over 200,000 old books, their spines glinting with gold in the rows and rows of shelves. I wander up and down the length of the room, peering at books from behind the roped-off areas and regarding the delicate open pages of ancient books in glass cabinets. I snap a photo of the full length of the Long Room, catching Holly in the frame in her Santa hat. It is one of my favourite photos of the holiday.

Afterwards we visit the Book of Kells exhibition for a viewing of a manuscript, which is known as 'a cultural treasure of Ireland.' One of the most visited attractions in Dublin and thought to have been crafted around 800 AD, the Book of Kells is a gospel manuscript illustrated on vellum (calf skin) with incredibly detailed and colourful drawings. Originally kept in the Abbey of Kells, a monastery in Kells in County Meath, it has been stored at Trinity College since the mid-seventeenth century.

There are only a few pages of the ancient volume open for public viewing, but the exhibition is vibrant and shows much more. The pages we are allowed to view are full of Christian icons, Celtic crosses, people, animals, mythical beasts, and more. With miniature drawings as well as full-page illuminations, it is bright with colour, detailed, and beautiful.

Then it's time to get ready for our 'evening of food, folklore, and fairies' at the Brazen Head, the oldest pub in Ireland, which was established in 1198. I'm so excited about this! What could be better than the wonderful combination of food, folklore, and fairies?

This night at the Brazen Head pub has been voted the 'Number 1 Nightlife Entertainment' by Trip Advisor, but that's not the only reason I booked it. I love myth and legend, fantasy and storytelling, and we're in Ireland, a hub of ancient mythology, fairies, sprites, and all things fantastical, so as soon as I found out about this dinner months ago, it was booked.

We rock up to the pub and are shown upstairs to a large but cosy and candlelit dining room. We're served drinks and shown the menu, and before long, singers begin to entertain us with lively Irish songs, like 'Whiskey in the Jar.'

Jonny the storyteller then regales us with stories of Irish life, politics, potatoes, famines, immigration, and of how the Irish still won't build over a fairy ring or fairy tree if they can help it—you don't want to upset the fairies! We hear magical tales wonderfully told of fairy and folklore, and from kids to grandparents, everyone is mesmerised by these mystical tales told theatrically with humour and intrigue. Jonny is witty and engaging, and it's such a great way to finish our time in Dublin!

We keep an eye out on the way back to the hotel for dachshunds, any dachshunds, especially ones with a leprechaun upon their backs, but to the kids' great disappointment, we don't see any. Come on, Dublin! Anthony is still in the lead and on track to take out the trophy.

(21)

BOSTON, USA

Date: December 19
Location: Dublin – Boston
Nights: 3
Dachshunds so far: 46

Friendly Faces

Our 4:00 am pre-booked airport transfer was a delightfully Irish experience after one taxi turns up for seven people and seven suitcases. Another taxi is called, but there is still some bewilderment about how our cases are going to fit. The taxi driver looks at us for some kind of explanation, and Anthony and David end up packing most of the cases into the two cars.

As the bags are maneuvered into the taxis, I prompt the kids to look around for one last look for the elusive mythical phenomenon that is a leprechaun riding a dachshund. But none are seen.

After twelve hours of transit, a 4:00 am pick-up, and a six-hour time difference, we arrive to a snow-covered Boston.

Snow, people.

SNOW.

Snow covers mostly everything, cars, boats, rooflines, and roads. It's sprinkled through trees and piled up around driveways and paths, and it's *awesome*. I'm pretty happy to be having one more snow experience. And it's a good one. The broad window in our Marriott Tudor Wharf apartment overlooks the Boston skyline, the Inner Harbor, and the big snowdrifts surrounding the hotel. It's so pretty.

We're super excited to soon be meeting up with our best friends, Heidi, Anthony, and their kids, Jay, Isabelle, and Ryan. We are only days away from seeing the rest of the family in New York City. Our party of seven will soon become twelve and then grow to twenty-six. For a few days, with our friends from Minnesota, Kayla and Kelsey, we will be twenty-eight!

The hotel receptionist advises us our friends have arrived but are exploring, so we do the same. We can't wait to see them, especially Anthony. He has been too long away from his best friend of the same name, Anthony. Although he's not feeling well, he can't keep the excited grin from his face. The kids are desperate for other children to hang out with. They've already advised me on a few occasions they love us, but you know, boring adults and all that. And as much as we love and adore our parents, Anthony and I are looking forward to some chilled out time with our mates.

We set out in our Santa hats into the snow, and the kids immediately begin making snowballs for a fight with Anthony and David. David and Anthony dodge icy snow, and there is plenty of laughter. They're not nearly as fast at throwing snowballs as Buddy the Elf, but they try their best.

The dachshund spotting begins, but I'm not so positive a dachshund would venture out into the snow. At home, Charlie will bury himself amongst his blankets at the first sign of chilly weather and has to be physically removed from his bed and forced to go outside for a pee, and Coco was much the same.

Perhaps Northern Hemisphere dachshunds are different? They must be much more acclimatised than Southern Hemisphere dachshunds, especially dachshunds who live in a climate where winter can sometimes mean clear, sunny days of fifteen to eighteen degrees Celsius (sixty to sixty-five Fahrenheit). Even then it's hard to get them to put their precious paws on the cold, wet grass.

It's beginning to darken, and the lights of Boston twinkle as we wander across the Charles River into Boston proper. The river is opaque with thin ice. We wander around the Italian Quarter and the harbour's edge, dodging slippery ice and puddles. Mum's knee is playing up, and Maree and David certainly don't want to have a fall, so after a while, we give up and head back to the apartment to find that our friends are back.

Excitement follows, especially from Ryan, their youngest, who has been counting down the days until he saw Sam. There are hugs and kisses and lots of talking as we catch up after not seeing them for a few months. We share our stupid gift of Santa suit onesies that they now have to fit in their overfull suitcases. How's that for a gift? Five sleeping bag-sized gifts that won't fit in your bag! Nice friends we are! They love them though, and the kids jump straight into them.

The kids race back and forth between rooms, playing games and talking. We catch up on news and head downstairs to the complimentary dinner offered by the hotel, which is great for us weary travellers. It is a pretty impressive spread of hamburgers, soft drinks, tea, coffee, chocolate chip cookies, brownies, and coleslaw.

To bed!

Super Duck, Meet Rubber Ducky

After a scavenger hunt Advent, our party of twelve all purchase hop-on, hop-off trolley tickets from the hotel reception, which includes a Duck Tour in the Boston Harbor on an amphibious vehicle.

After the kids have a quick snowball fight in the powdery snow outside the hotel, we follow the instructions from the receptionist to the trolley bus stop, which we can't find! But the twelve of us have a nice forty-five-minute walk around the navy yards and back to where we started. In this whole process of trying to find the bus stop, speedy-walking Anthony appears to have forgotten his need for speed of the last nine weeks. He walks along with his mate, *strolling almost*, with the party of twelve stretched behind. The oldies, I'm sure, would have loved this pace over the past couple of months!

Eventually a bus comes, and we all hop on and then hop back off not long after at the Super Duck depot, which we wandered past on our walk. Too funny! We board the big yellow boat for a tour around Boston Harbor.

The Super Duck drives straight into the water with a splash. It's a clear day, with blue sky and bright sun, and it's nice to see Boston from afar. Our humorous driver and guide fills us in on some of the history of Boston, its buildings, the old navy yard, and shows us how much of Boston is reclaimed land. We cruise past the Charlestown Navy Yard and the USS Constitution, an old navy ship, and one by one, each of the kids have a turn sitting near the captain.

There is a loud call, 'Dachshund!' from Anthony. I turn in my seat, and lo and behold there is a dachshund on a wharf in-between the navy yards and our hotel. Unbelievable!

Dachshund Spotting Total:
Anthony 29, Holly 4.5, David 4, Sam 3.5, Maree 3, Lisa 2, Mum 1

The tour ends back at the Super Duck depot where David takes a photo with the Rotary rubber ducky together with the huge amphibious vehicle.

History Lessons with Corey . . . or Martin

After the duck tour, we hop back on the bus for the red loop around Boston. With other kids along, the kids aren't quite so bored on city tours, mainly because they are so busy laughing and chatting. They're probably not listening so much, but then neither am I! There are more people to talk to, so less time for listening. I have to say though, the bus driver is much more entertaining than most tour guides. His name is Corey, unless you don't like him, in which case his name is Martin. Ha!

Firstly, we see the Bunker Hill Monument, the site of a bloody battle fought against the British in 1775 in the early stages of the American War of Independence. We cruise past Boston City Hall, a long, quite unusual looking building, which looks a little out of place, and the Old State House where the Declaration of Independence was proclaimed from its balcony on July 4, 1776.

Next up is Boston Commons, a huge city park and the oldest in the country, having been a city park since 1634.

After a full loop we hop off at State Street at Faneuil Hall, the meeting place of colonial Boston. Next to it is the festive-looking Faneuil Marketplace, which looks like a great place to feed the hordes. We lunch in the expansive food hall, raid a lolly shop for Gobstoppers, Razzles, and lollies, buy two pairs of dachshund socks (which I try to claim as a sighting—denied), and look through a beautiful Christmas decoration shop where I buy yet another decoration for our tree in New York City.

We wander back to the hotel through the melting snow, sidestep icy cold puddles, and comment that the grey slush isn't so pretty. The snow is definitely losing its appeal, and unfortunately for us, the weather is crisp and sunny with no sign of rain or snowflakes in the air. Maree and David head back to the hotel for a rest while the rest of us continue to the USS Constitution.

We line up for a tour and are told we need ID to board the ship, which is OK for us but not for Anthony, who, no matter how many times I suggest he should carry ID on him, does not have his. He is not allowed on the ship and turns back to the hotel to grab it while we continue on the tour. I'm not sure why they insist on ID, as when I'm ushered through the security checkpoint, mine is not even glanced at.

Called the Constitution by George Washington, but nicknamed 'Old Ironsides' because of her ability to stay afloat during the War of 1812 against the English and her allies, she is the oldest naval ship still in service in the world.

A navy officer takes us below deck to show us the cannons and explain how the ship was specially built to support their weight. We learn what sailors ate every day for breakfast, lunch, and dinner (salted meat), what they drank (rum), and where they slept (hammocks). He explains the story of how the USA defeated the English by separating us into groups and making us yell out, 'Boom!' when imaginary cannons are being fired. Our side (the English) is hopeless at it and loses the battle. Surprise, surprise, the USA wins!

When we climb the narrow stairs up to the deck, we find Anthony standing there. He went all the way back to the hotel, grabbed his ID, and walked straight back onto the USS Constitution without being asked for it! Go figure!

He is a little bit cranky, as he was standing on deck for ages because he wasn't allowed to go down to the lower deck 'unattended,' even though there are about six people on deck that could have 'attended' him down. If we ever go back to Boston, I'll tell you where Anthony won't be going . . .

After a short walk across the Charlestown Bridge, we end up in Boston's Little Italy for dinner. We make our way down the narrow streets with restaurants in every other old building. There are a lot of lights and decorations and plenty of people out for dinner. It's only now we think we should have made a booking. The twelve of us are turned away from the first few restaurants, until finally one takes us in. I'm so glad I have three dinners already booked for the twenty-six of us in New York City. There is no way we could get in anywhere as a walk-in.

It is a great night, but there is enough food on the plates to feed a small country and way too much for all of us. We take home the leftovers in plastic containers. I'm sure there is enough there to feed all of us again tomorrow night.

Cambridge, Not Boston, Folks!

We wake and eat what the kids think is one of the best breakfasts ever as there is a make-your-own waffle maker. This hotel is a winner!

The boys want to check out Harvard and Fenway Park, so we hop back on our favourite hop-on, hop-off trolley bus and make our way to the Harvard Loop.

Our gravelly-voiced driver explains, in *the* broadest Bostonian accent I've heard so far, which I love, that Cambridge is a *separate* city from Boston and not part of the greater Boston area. And in case you are wondering, Ben Affleck and Matt Damon are *not* from Boston as quoted in the press, but from Cambridge. It seems to mean a great deal to the driver. Get it right, people! They're from Cambridge, OK!

We pass MIT, the Massachusetts Institute of Technology or as the tour guide tells us, Millionaires in Training, and then we continue to Harvard. As we cruise into Cambridge, the driver advises us that our IQs have risen and surely we feel smarter as we near Harvard. It didn't seem to work on me, but Heidi and I decided since we have now been to Harvard, we could add it to our list of schooling achievements.

Founded in 1636, Harvard is the oldest school in America and one of the most prestigious in the world. We wander through the grounds, and the kids race around having snowball fights. Sam and Ryan do their best to do some sledding with the small red sled that

Heidi and Anthony bought. The snow is half-melted with grass and dirt showing, and there isn't a hill to be found, but they still try!

A sudden dachshund call is made. Of course, it's Anthony, who else? He points toward the statue of John Harvard, the founder of the college and its first benefactor, and sure enough, there is a brown, smooth haired dachshund with a very festive red coat.

Dachshund Spotting Total:
Anthony 30, Holly 4.5, David 4, Sam 3.5, Maree 3, Lisa 2, Mum 1

I swear we don't see many other dogs! Is it that we can *only* see dachshunds? I'm not kidding when I say we haven't seen many other dogs. I'm sure there are other breeds of dogs walking around right in front of our eyes, but it's dachshunds we *want* to see, so that's what we're seeing, or rather, Anthony is seeing.

Unbeknownst to us, are we drawing dachshunds to us? We imagine them, we see them trotting by in our minds, so they appear on wharves, parks, in cafes to sit on the feet of Grandma, by riverbanks and beaches, and in handbags. I am pondering way too deeply on this, but I do wonder. We are up to forty-eight dachshunds now. I never thought we would see this many.

Holly asks how many days it is till we see Charlie. The answer: twenty-one. 'Not long now,' I say. She nods, and we hug.

'Are we still getting a puppy?' she checks. She's asked this a few times.

I nod, and she races off to join the snowball fight. I haven't looked for a couple of days, but my secret puppy search hasn't been going so well. Not one single website I've been on says they have any pups available. Emails need to be sent, enquiries made, as not all breeders list available dogs on their websites. But I'm not ready to make that extra step yet. I need to be home, I think, because regardless of the truth, regardless of Coco's ashes resting at home, regardless of the jacaranda tree we've had planted to remember her by, it still doesn't seem real.

The two Anthonys amble ahead together, enjoying each other's company, and Heidi and I follow along chatting like best friends do about anything and everything. Mum, Maree, and David are close by but hanging back, I think, so we can hang out with our friends, like they would if Anthony and I were teenagers. The three grandparents laugh and chat easily, good friends when the trip started but even greater friends now.

We pose for photos before the large entrance gates of Harvard, but it's cold, so we slip into the Starbucks in Harvard Square to grab much needed coffees and hot chocolates.

Ball Time

Let's go Red Sox, *let's go!* That's right, it's time for Fenway Park, the home of the Boston Red Sox, and the two Anthonys are excited. The two grandmas not so much, and as we hop off the bus to change loops, they stay on, waving to us with smiles. I see more coffee, cake, and possibly shopping in their immediate future. David stays with us, and soon enough we are disembarking at the ballpark.

We book our tour, and before long, we're taken into the grandstand to sit in the old wooden seats and hear about some of the history of the Red Sox from our guide. We hear stories of Babe Ruth being sold to the Yankees and the losing streak of the Red

Sox, which I find out, went for eighty-six years until they finally won in 2004.

We wander through the change rooms, take a seat in the press room, look upon the bronze Hall of Fame pictures, and hear about the Green Monster, a wall built in the 1930s to stop balls from hitting shopfronts outside, but mainly to stop people sitting on rooftops and watching the games for free. When we exit the park, an elderly man shows us his chunky championship rings on his fingers and describes them as 'chick magnets' while he leans down close to Heidi's fifteen-year-old daughter, who, rightly so, looks a little alarmed.

The Cheers bar, or the inspiration for the Cheers bar to put it rightly, is our next stop on the bus loop. We go down the stairs and wind our way through the front bar to the backroom past plenty of Cheers memorabilia on the way. It's very busy but it doesn't take us long to get a table. I'm excited to see it! I know it's cheesy, but I loved that show, as did Anthony. Every time I think about it, it reminds me of younger days at home with my sister and parents gathered around the TV to watch it. The lunch of beer, burgers, hotdogs, and stew is delicious.

Afterwards we visit the gift shop, one Anthony is finally happy to go in, and we buy coasters, a bottle opener, and a Christmas decoration. Then we head upstairs to the replica bar. It is roped off, so we can't go and sit where Frasier sat or anything, but it's still pretty cool to see.

A quiet night in follows with our leftover food that feeds all of us. Mum snaps a photo of all nine of us in our Santa suit onesies before it's time for another pack-up and bed.

I can't wait to see everyone in New York City, especially my sister!

Bye-bye, Boston.

Hello, New York City!

(22)

NEW YORK CITY, USA

Date: *December 22*
Location: *Boston — New York City*
Nights: *10*
Dachshunds so far: *48*

Watching and Loving

I t's a quick Advent this morning of little Kinder chocolates, but I remind the kids about their 'The Twelve Days of Christmas' song challenge. Not that Holly needs reminding. She downloaded the song in early December and has been practicing every day. Sam? Not so much, and Holly is starting to become concerned about Sam still receiving this much talked about mystery gift without completing the challenge correctly, which is singing the whole song off by heart.

Mum is at the door with her bags packed as usual, and Maree and David have already been down to let us know they're ready. Retirees are the best at being on time. Actually, they are really good at being half an hour early. I will learn this skill as I age, hopefully. All of them are excited, as are we. New York City for Christmas and a week at Disney World with the whole family is beyond cool, and every day I remind myself how lucky we are to be experiencing this.

As Anthony and I prepare to leave Boston, our sisters, Karen and Gemma, and their families are preparing to leave Washington, DC to meet us in New York City. Anthony's brother, Chris, and his family are in-flight right now on their way from Australia.

I can't help but think of Dad as Christmas nears, as I'm sure most people do when regular family events roll around each year. Another year has disappeared without him. How does this happen? How has another year gone by, and we haven't seen him?

In those first weeks after Dad's death, it was awful to comprehend that I would *never* see him again, never receive that big bear hug that he was so good at, never hear his laugh again or get caught listening to a long conversation about petrol consumption while towing a caravan—I even miss that, and it was the most boring conversation in the world. And then one year passes and another, and I wonder where that time has gone. This is an experience he would have loved. Half the time when I think about Dad, it's not about how much I miss him, it's how sad it makes me that he is missing out.

He may be watching over us—and I hope he is, even though I'm unsure of what I believe when it comes to the afterlife, but one thing is for sure, death makes you start to think about it. As we pack up today to go and meet the family, I hope he *is* watching and loving every minute of it.

Just Right

It is a balmy nineteen degrees Celsius in New York City when we arrive, foiling my plans for a white Christmas, but there is snow on the horizon, the weather websites assure me. After our arrival Anthony and I begin the long process of checking in all six of the rooms, so when everyone arrives, they are all set.

The hotel I chose, after hours and hours of searching, days in fact, is the TRYP Times Square South. After my exhaustive searching, which included a detailed spreadsheet, I'm really pleased to find that it is perfect. I didn't realise how nervous I was until we arrived. I am jittery, and it's not until we check in and see the rooms that I take a deep breath and calm down. I wanted the hotel to be 'just right,' and it is.

We all wait downstairs at the bar in the foyer of the hotel, another big plus for the hotel. A gathering place within the hotel building was a must when I was looking for hotels. Not all have a bar, but with this many people, I wanted somewhere for people to go for a quick drink without walking half a block down the road.

Everyone is excited, especially Maree, David, and Mum, and we all keep watching the door. My sister Karen is first with Bruce and the boys, Matthew and Jason. And not long after, Anthony's sister Gemma arrives with David and their children, Jacob, Abby, and Hayley. Hugs and kisses and excitement follow.

It's so exciting and is as I predicted with my fancy mathematical equation: Excitement seeing the family in New York City = Christmas market excitement times infinity. We have one more family to arrive, Anthony's brother, Chris, his wife, Trudy, and their three boys, Jack, Nathan, and Max. They will arrive late after we are all in bed, so their keys are left at reception.

The new arrivals are shown to their rooms, and we relax in the bar over a drink to catch up and work out some of the activities for the ten days. I am an over-planner with holidays and already have a few things booked in for the whole group (all prearranged and discussed with families prior), but I want everyone to be able to do what they want in New York City. So, there will be times when everyone goes separate ways. It is, I think a *very* important part of the success of a family holiday. Not *everything* has to be done together.

Anthony grabs a sheet of paper and starts putting together a rough itinerary for the week. I leave him to it—for once not feeling the burning need to be involved in every little detail of the holiday. I want to sit back with the family and catch up and relax.

Before long tummies begin to grumble, and it occurs to me that I didn't think about dinner for tonight. I have three dinners pre-booked: Christmas Day, Anthony's birthday, and New Year's Eve, but not tonight. Takeaway is easy, walk anywhere in New York City, and you'll find a quick meal, but we all wanted to go out to dinner and sit and enjoy a meal together. But you simply can't wander out with a party of twenty-one and expect to be seated at a restaurant. Not two days before Christmas.

Anthony and I begin to ring around, but we don't have much luck with the first three restaurants. 'Twenty-one?' they ask, 'And you want to come now?'

Movin' the Gaggle

Finally someone says yes, and we set out into the streets. It's cold now and busy with people. It becomes apparent as our line of walkers stretches almost a whole block that twenty-one people cannot walk in a clumped group all at the same pace. Our ages range from five to seventy, and again I notice that Anthony doesn't seem to care anymore about the pace, or if he does, he's not saying anything. I feel like he's been irritated for nine weeks about the walking pace and now nothing. G-r-r-r.

We walk for six long blocks, all hungry and eager for dinner, when someone in the front, I won't mention any names, realises that we are walking the WRONG way. Ha! After a quick phone call to the restaurant to assure them we were still coming, we turn around and retrace our steps. Twelve blocks later we arrive. The grandparents sit down eagerly, and Hayley, the youngest niece, is as fresh as a daisy, having been piggy-backed nearly the entire way. Nice work, Hayley. With her bad knee I reckon Mum wouldn't have minded a piggyback.

After dinner, we stop at Macy's Christmas window displays on the way back, and the children gather to look at the festive scenes. As we make our way through the streets, the Empire State Building shines brightly between the high-rise buildings lit up for Christmas in red and green.

Highline, 9/11 Memorial & the Radio City Christmas Spectacular

We awake excited about our first full day in New York City, and after welcoming the last lot of Fleetwoods to New York City, Chris and Trudy and the boys, who are still exhausted from their flight, half the group makes its way downtown to visit the 9/11 Memorial via the Highline, a 1.5-mile walkway that winds above the streets on an elevated, disused railroad.

Initially set for demolition, it has taken years of work to transform this old line into a linear parkway. And even though it only runs for a mile and a half, it's a nice way to walk the streets above the traffic and exhaust fumes. It's fresh and clean, and except the few evergreens and the huge holly tree, which Holly poses for a photo before, most of the garden is winter-worn and bare, but it's definitely worth a walk along the paved track.

No dachshunds have been spotted yet, even though we're looking.

The Highline ends all too soon, and we descend back to the street and into the subway to travel the rest of the way downtown to the memorial. It's raining when we emerge from the subway, and hoods are up as we make our way to the 9/11 site. The memorial is very moving, and the design is brilliant. With two large, square pools located in the footprint of where the Twin Towers stood, water flows smoothly downwards into the small square void in the centre.

I'm mesmerised by the water. I can't see the bottom and find myself on tiptoes trying to see farther in. The names of each victim, all 2,983, are inscribed in the bronze parapet surrounding each pool. It's so sad to see all those names and the stark white roses against the dark colour of the memorial. For such a busy, noisy city there is calm at the memorial; everyone is very respectful of all it represents. It is hard not to be.

The afternoon activity is one I am excited about, the Radio City Christmas Spectacular. I've watched a few too many YouTube clips of this show, so I know it's going to be, as its name suggests, spectacular. Radio City Hall is famous for its high-kicking Rockettes but also for its Christmas show, which has been playing there every year since 1932.

We arrive early for the afternoon show, nearly all of us walking in one big group, a gaggle of children, parents, and grandparents spread across a city block. As usual, five-year-old Hayley has convinced one of the teenage girls or boys to carry her on their back or shoulders. She is so terribly cute that she gets away with it every time. Gemma reminds her she has legs, but Hayley only smiles in response from her perch atop Sam's shoulders.

Soon we are inside the beautiful Art Deco theatre and seated up high. The lights dim, the music begins, and the voice of Santa narrates the show. Soon the famous Rockettes, dressed as reindeer, dance onto the stage pulling Santa in his sleigh. They are so in-sync with their perfectly timed kicks, it's unbelievable. Next they tap dance through 'The Twelve Days of Christmas,' so Holly thinks Sam will finally learn the song for the song challenge tonight when he hasn't practiced all month. Unfair!

The stage is then filled with a Christmas tree and presents, and a girl dances with a nutcracker teddy in the Radio City version of 'The Nutcracker' before the Rockettes are back in all their glittered finery. To finish up the show, is the nativity in beautiful colour, celebrated with carols, wise men, and real live camels, all arriving to give glory to the newborn king. The show is absolutely incredible although for some of the older boys, the sixteen- and seventeen-year-olds, the show struggled to hold their attention. One fell asleep.

Then it's time for last minute Christmas shopping and a Christmas tree purchase, which is a tiny, little green plant with such soft branches it is hard to hang all the Christmas decorations I'd collected on our travels on it, but we manage. It is quite possibly the most pathetic tree of all time, but we love it!

Christmas Eve

Christmas Eve is such a clear, beautiful day that it is in no way a good indicator for a white Christmas, but Weather.com says there will be snow, and just quietly, I have my fingers crossed.

We jump on the subway, twenty-two of us, and head downtown to the Staten Island Ferry Terminal to board the ferry. It's really chilly but fabulous to be out on the water. The city's vista is stunning. We pass Ellis Island, where for millions of immigrants, it was their first taste of America, and the Statue of Liberty reaching for the sky. I snap photos of cousins holding hands, kids snuggling with Maree and David, Anthony leaning on the rail, and Mum, Karen, Bruce, and the boys sitting close together on the deck.

Half an hour later we dock at Staten Island and walk along the boardwalk. A smiling David makes every child pose with the yellow rubber ducky, and they happily do so. It gets around, that duck. Many more photos are taken with the skyline of New York City as the backdrop. I cuddle with my Mum and my sister, and we grin at the camera. Dad is not here, but we have each other, and that is a good thing.

Heidi's Anthony wonders where Coney Island is, so my Anthony heads back to the ferry terminal to ask. He has the biggest grin on his face as he walks back, having asked possibly the dumbest question ever when he informs us all that Coney Island is in Brooklyn and *not* on Staten Island. Ba-ha-ha-ha-ha! We are such tourists!

Afterwards, we walk from the ferry port to the Brooklyn Bridge and plan to walk across it to Brooklyn, just to say we've done it. Apparently that's a thing. It is busy with people, cranky bike riders, and artists selling their paintings.

When we arrive back to the hotel, Maree announces with a big grin that there's been a double dachshund sighting. Well, she saw one and David (son-in-law) saw the other, and as he's not in the competition, Maree is allocated the points for both. And, there we have it—we've hit fifty dachshunds!

Dachshund Spotting Total:
Anthony 30, Maree 5, Holly 4.5, David 4, Sam 3.5, Lisa 2, Mum 1

Let the Festive Fun Begin!

The four of us get into the Christmas mood by dressing in our Santa suit onesies, and we do a late last Advent for the year. The kids gear up for their 'The Twelve Days of Christmas' song challenge. Sam groans his way through the whole, long song. It's painful to listen to. Holly whips through it quickly, and they both earn their super prize, a mini Bluetooth speaker each and an M&M-filled candy cane. I'm not a hundred percent sure Sam thought singing the song was worth it.

As soon as everyone is back, Anthony's planned room and hall Christmas Eve party kicks off. Our rooms are at the end of a hallway, and we prop doors open and weave between the rooms. It's time for Santa suit onesies, takeaway pizza and pasta, beer and wine, and family and friends to get together for a few hours before Santa arrives. We laugh and chat, and when Maree rings Nana, her ninety-six-year-old mother, all twenty-six of us say a very loud,

'Merry Christmas!' to her, which results in the guy down the hall telling us to keep it down! Oops.

Then it's time for our Christmas Skype date with Charlie. The four of us crowd around the computer and watch him leap around with his tongue lolling and tail wagging. He looks happy and cared for and seems back to his normal self. It is *so* good to see him.

Suddenly there is a snow sighting from Maree, Trudy, and Karen, so a few of us traipse downstairs in our Santa onesies and out the front of the hotel to check it out. We see a flake or two, maybe three, so that means IT SNOWED ON CHRISTMAS EVE! Don't tell me it didn't.

We settle into the two queen beds in our onesies with Heidi, Anthony, and the kids and watch *Elf*. For the first time in many years of *Elf*-watching on Christmas Eve, I can't seem to keep my eyes open. It's been a big day. Afterwards the kids lay out their stockings before our tiny tree, and Holly prepares the milk and cookies for Santa.

Happy Christmas to all, and to all a good night!

Christmas Day in New York City

I wake on Christmas morning, and everyone is still asleep. The first thing I do is tiptoe to the window to see if there is snow! Nope! Well, shit. After last night's three snowflakes, I thought that maybe there would be some snow this morning, or even a sprinkling, but there's nothing. There is a cold front coming though, and snow. But when? Not today, I know that much! Even though no snow has come, Santa has! Our Christmas tree has presents at its base. Yay!

Everyone has a personal little Christmas in their rooms, before Mum, Karen, Bruce, and the boys join us in our room to celebrate.

Then we see Maree, David, and everyone else, and the doors to hotel rooms are propped open again. We all celebrate with people roaming between rooms, calling Christmas greetings, and hugging.

What's a good thing to do in New York City on Christmas Day? We decide that's ice-skating in Central Park, so after a breakfast of bagels and cream cheese, many of us do just that. We rug up and head out into the cold, and it *is* cold.

I'd printed a map of department store Christmas window displays, so as we walk, we make our way down Fifth Avenue past Lord and Taylor and Saks Fifth Avenue, and there are people crowded around each window. There are people everywhere, plenty with Santa hats on like us, and plenty of smiling faces.

Holly and I link arms as we turn into Rockefeller Plaza. We draw in a deep breath, like Buddy the Elf, as we see the big tree. It's miraculous! We all make our way down through the busy plaza. The queue to skate on the Rockefeller Rink is ginormous, which I already knew it would be. I already did my research about it—not only are we not waiting hours in line, none of us are willing to pay the price to skate there—so after watching for a while, we continue to Central Park to the Wollman Rink, taking in the Bergdorf and Goodman window displays on the way.

The Wollman Rink in Central Park is large and has the city skyline as a stunning backdrop. It's crowded, but the lines don't take too long, and Holly and I hold hands as we glide around the ice. One of my cute nieces joins us, and we skate around for a while, with Sam zooming by with cousins and friends on his heels. I grin at Holly. 'I can't believe we're here, in New York City, ice skating on Christmas Day. It's pretty cool.' All the rest are waiting up top at the viewing platform, and we wave to them.

We stroll through the park, past the Central Park Zoo, and watch the kids climb rocks and race about. The park is absolutely beautiful with meandering pathways, rolling green lawns, and horse and carriages clip-clopping by. We are buying roasted nuts and hot dogs when Anthony makes his first dachshund call for New York City.

I turn and just ahead is the cutest black, longhaired dachshund, wearing a festive green coat and a red scarf with bells on it. Oh, this makes us miss Charlie so much. 'Only 19 days until we see Charlie,' I tell the kids. Tears sting at my eyes. Home means no Coco. Home means really facing she's gone.

Dachshund Spotting Total:
Anthony 31, Maree 5, Holly 4.5, David 4, Sam 3.5, Lisa 2, Mum 1

Then minutes later Anthony spots another one near the Central Park Lake. This dachshund is brown and tan with black-tipped ears in a red and green coat, and it's a snappy one. G-r-r-r! But then the owner picks it up and allows the kids to pat it.

Dachshund Spotting Total:
Anthony 32, Maree 5, Holly 4.5, David 4, Sam 3.5, Lisa 2, Mum 1

We walk all the way back to the hotel, blocks and blocks, and get ready for Christmas dinner at the Rock Center Cafe. I want to go early as no matter how many times in the last four months I confirmed this booking, I am still a bit worried that something is going to go wrong. So half the group leaves early, and we make our

237

way along Fifth Avenue to Rockefeller Plaza. And isn't that the worst mistake in the world.

The closer we get to the plaza, there are more and more crowds, and it's so packed we can't even get in there. It appears that half the population of New York City is stuffed into this square. We were only here a few hours ago when I leaned over the high side of the ice rink and pointed out the Rock Center Cafe to Mum.

I know where it is, but we can't get there. On the building opposite the plaza, a music and light show begins, and more crowds press in. It's so busy we are hardly moving, and I ask Anthony to wait at the corner of Fifth Avenue to catch the rest of the group. It is insane, and no one we ask seems to be able to help us find a way to get to the cafe, until finally I ask a security guard who points us in the direction of a lift that will take us down to the restaurant, but it takes twenty-five minutes to get to through the crowds. And the lift? It has a very long queue.

'Is there no other way to get to this restaurant?' I think.

I find out later that there is another way, but right at that moment, nobody seems to be able tell us that information even though we ask a few times. Slowly, slowly we move up the queue and finally make it down to the restaurant to find Chris, Trudy, and the boys waiting outside, wondering where we were. They came in from another way and walked straight in. How I wish I knew that.

Thank goodness we left early as we are only five minutes late, but the drama isn't quite over. Despite booking for twenty-six people four months ago, despite a confirmation email in November and another a few days ago, and despite their having our credit card details securing the booking, they act surprised when I say that the booking is for twenty-six people. How is that possible?

I am one of those people who brings a printout of emails and bookings with me. I hand it to them and show them *quite clearly* that I booked this months ago. It is only after one staff member looks and then another is called to look at my confirmation that they start to look like they may provide us with some tables. I fail to understand how our booking is not in their system. It is beyond my comprehension. I decide not to remind them that every single email assures me window seats. I think that may confuse them even further. I am calm still, but shaking inside. I would very much like a big glass of wine.

They take us over to one long table and two round ones, but we are still short seats. The staff scramble and find four chairs and squish them onto the table. I am so busy running around making sure people are seated that when I walk back to Anthony, who is standing with Anthony and Heidi, we realise there are no seats for us. I grab the waiter and ask for another table. 'I'm sorry,' the waiter says, 'there aren't any.'

But over her shoulder I spy a freshly set table for four by the window. 'How about that one?' I suggest. The waitress shakes her head and attempts to say no, but she doesn't get the chance.

'We're sitting there,' I announce and defiantly march over to sit in a chair. The others follow and sit down.

I take a deep breath. Wine please!

It is then that the four of us realise that we are seated on our own a few tables away from everyone else and our kids. We grin. Is that wrong? It's Christmas dinner, and our kids are over yonder. We four look at each other and try not to grin too much. We didn't mean for this to happen, but my, oh my, this is fabulous! And sorry to Karen and Bruce and Mum who seem to have ended up with all of our kids. However, at that point, after an hour of craziness, I need this. I give the kids a wave, take a deep breath, and sip on the wine that has just turned up.

Despite the initial terrible service, the Rock Center Cafe redeems itself. With the ice rink bordering the windows and the ginormous Rockefeller tree spanning high above, it is an atmospheric place to enjoy Christmas dinner, especially when the rink clears and we watch a marriage proposal on the ice. The three-course meal is absolutely outstanding, everyone is happy and smiling, and at one point I have to blink away tears. After so much planning, our Christmas in New York City all came together. And it's awesome.

Merry Christmas!

Boxing Day, A Day of Wins

It's Boxing Day today, a British and Australian holiday, but more importantly, it's Anthony's birthday. I want to make it special for him, as without his hard work over the years, this trip would not have happened for any of us. Although he doesn't like a fuss and is not one to want a birthday party, I've booked us all in at the New York City Beer Company for dinner. But first, there are birthday presents and visits from all the family to give birthday best wishes. We give Anthony the crystal dachshund that I've been carrying around since Prague.

Today is another day of exploring New York City. Some are taking carriage rides around Central Park, others to the Empire State Building or the Natural History Museum.

For us four and Anthony and Heidi, second-time visitors to New York City, we decide to go to the Top of the Rock, the observation deck of Rockefeller Center.

On the way I have a double dachshund spotting in a jewellery shop—two tiny dachshund pendants, one black and one tan, just like Charlie and Coco. Anthony denies the call, but I buy the dogs.

It is freezing on the Top of the Rock, and as we look over the city, it starts to snow. It is light at first and then slightly heavier, enough to leave a light covering on the ground and eddy around our faces. The kids catch snowflakes on their tongues. We stand there grinning in the sparking snowfall. 'Happy birthday, Anthony,' I think. I will never forget standing up there with snow drifting around us on Anthony's birthday.

The New York Beer Company proves to be a fabulous spot for a group of twenty-six people for several reasons.

—After booking three months ago and a couple of confirmation emails, they are expecting me, and when such a massive group enters the foyer, I am greeted by name.

—It is a bar.

—They are really flexible about kids in the bar. Even thirteen kids.

—There is plenty of room for all of us.

—And this is the best part: there is a circular, high top bar table with six stools and a beer tap in the middle with four different beers. The look of glee on Anthony's face is priceless. Best birthday bar ever.

Booking win!

To finish the wonderful day, a big group of us heads to the cinema to see *Anchorman 2*, a *slightly* inappropriate movie for Holly and a couple of the other younger teenagers. OK, highly inappropriate in parts, but *Anchorman 1* is a favourite movie in our house. For years, we just did a few fast-forwards at some of the choice moments accompanied by the kids' hands over their eyes. Yes, I'm a bad parent.

What an absolutely fabulous day.

Minnesota Twins

From the moment we wake and dress each day, our door and the doors to the surrounding rooms are propped open, and friends and family chat about the day's activities over tea and coffee as the kids play.

Today a whole tribe of the family is visiting the Intrepid Sea, Air & Space Museum, a military museum on an aircraft carrier, and the others are exploring the city, but the four of us are meeting our friends who are flying in from Minnesota. Party of twenty-eight in the house!

Kayla and Kelsey are sisters we met in Australia who were out for three months on a student-teacher exchange. Kayla was billeted to our house through the kids' school, and we've stayed in touch. I'm pretty excited to be seeing them again, as honestly, I didn't think we ever would.

Kayla and Kelsey arrive with the biggest smiles, and having never been to New York City, they are super excited, to put it mildly! They unpack, and we hit the streets, heading to where most tourists want to go first—Times Square.

It's the twenty-seventh of December today and creeping closer to New Year's Eve, but I was not expecting the crowds, not yet. Long barriers line the streets in Times Square, funneling the crowds into a smaller space on the streets, leaving only a small gap at street corners for crossing the road. Once we're in the press of people, it is mayhem and much more crowded than Rockefeller Plaza on

Christmas Day. At least at Rockefeller, most people were standing and watching the light show or the ice-skating, so we simply had to try and get through, but here we meet resistance. People are all going in different directions and are pushy, loud, and rough. One family links arms in a circle and barges through, not caring whom they knock over—it is awful. Welcome to New York City, ladies!

Regardless, we enjoy a great lunch at TGI Fridays with the girls, but it is the last time I plan to go to Times Square. I've done my research already, plenty of it. Times Square is *not* the place to be on New Year's Eve. One million people, hours of standing around and doing nothing, and no toilets. No thank you. As we depart the restaurant, I decide that Times Square is not the place to be even now, on the twenty-seventh of December.

While Kayla and Kelsey explore New York City, we hit Madison Square Garden with Chris, Trudy, Heidi, Anthony, and all the kids to see the New York Knicks play the Toronto Raptors. With a big orange finger, we cheer the Knicks on, and I absolutely love it. It's loud and noisy and exciting. Even though the Knicks lose, it's a great game.

No dachshunds spotted today. Come on, New York City, reveal your dachshunds to me!

More City Touring

I wake before everyone, but instead of writing the travel blog, I go down to Mum's room. I know she'll be awake, and I've missed her, as well as Maree and David, since we've met up with everyone. And even though we still catch up for afternoon wines, cups of tea, and chats, the fact that we were all doing different things in the last few days meant that I didn't see them quite as much. I knock on the door, and she answers. She is awake but still in her pyjamas, and I sit in bed with her and have a cup of tea.

When I sneak back to my room, doors are open and everyone is up. People move from room to room, chatting and working out who is doing what and who is joining whom for what activity. Kayla and Kelsey decide to see as much of the city as they can while they're here, so they have a big day planned. A few go together to the 9/11 Memorial while others explore Central Park, but for us— the two Anthonys decide we are going on a self-guided walking tour of Harlem.

The morning is spent walking the quiet streets of Harlem, visiting the Malcolm Shabazz Harlem Market, an African market on 52 West 116th Street, and wandering up to Morningside Park for the kids to play. On a day where we use the subway a lot, we travel uptown to see Yankee Stadium before heading back downtown for a big walk through Battery Park and the esplanade. The lovely esplanade edging the Hudson River proves to be a good decision, as within minutes there is a call from Anthony as we see a dapple dachshund. Minutes later Sam makes his own call. I can't see it at first, but ahead, amongst a group of people is a brown, longhaired dachshund. As usual the dachshund excitement is ridiculous.

Dachshund Spotting Total:
Anthony 33, Maree 5, Holly 4.5, Sam 4.5, David 4, Lisa 2, Mum 1

'How long is it until we see Charlie now, Mum?' Holly asks.
'Only fifteen days.'
'That's ages.'

'Well, the last seventy-three days have gone pretty quickly, haven't they?'

'Dachshund!' Anthony calls loudly.

A chocolate dachshund approaches with a friendly man in tow. We ask for a pat and have a cuddle with it. It's so cute!

Dachshund Spotting Total:

Anthony 34, Maree 5, Holly 4.5, Sam 4.5, David 4, Lisa 2, Mum 1

Rain, Rain Go Away

We choose possibly the worst day to see our first-ever NFL game, but we're still excited, although I'm sure Holly and Isabelle could think of a gazillion things they'd rather do. Others in the group have planned to visit the Top of the Rock and the Statue of Liberty, but thirteen of us, including Kayla and Kelsey and my brother-in-law Bruce and nephew Matthew, brave the chill and relentless rain, and head to Penn Station to board a shuttle bus out to New Jersey's MetLife Stadium to watch the New York Giants play. The bus depot is crowded with people, and we join a queue to find plenty of Australians in the line waiting with us. My head turns every time I hear an Aussie accent. They're everywhere!

Entering the car park, we see our first tailgate party, although it is possibly a little deflated with today's weather. What dedication to stand out in the rain and set up gazebos and BBQs in this weather. It's a pretty good effort! Cars and trucks crowd the car park, as do piles of discarded rubbish in the grimy grey slush of days-old snow. Ever heard of a trashcan? It's a round thing that trash goes in. See, I know my US lingo. Trash.

We head in, rain ponchos on, and spend *hours* in the rain. The two Anthonys may need to write the game report. But from me—

what game? I think there are some guys running around on the field below, but as the game progresses the stadium begins to empty—but do we leave too? No. We stick it out until the very end. I am soaked to the skin, as is everyone else. But what an experience!

Ducky Ties & Robin Sparkles

Even after such a freezing day, we pick up Kayla and Kelsey, and head out into the cold again to McGee's Pub, the inspiration for *How I Met Your Mother*. Since we are *HIMYM* tragics, Anthony and Sam are right into the theme of things, and both wear duckie ties like our favourite character, Barney Stinson.

When we exit the subway station, Holly makes a dachshund call. Ahead is a black, smooth haired dachshund in a checkered blue coat. She is so excited as it looks just like Charlie!

Dachshund Spotting Total:
Anthony 34, Maree 5, Holly 5.5, Sam 4.5, David 4, Lisa 2, Mum 1

The bar doesn't look much like the *HIMYM* bar, but we head in anyway. My biggest dilemma for the night is deciding which cocktail to get—the Naked Man, the Slutty Pumpkin, or the Robin Sparkles? I finally settle on the Robin Sparkles.

Pizza Pies, Please

Today it is time for the Brooklyn Pizza Tour. I'd seen this tour in a Sydney newspaper travel magazine, and Heidi and I decide it will be a winner, so twenty-two of us head off to meet the bus. As the bus rolls through Brooklyn, the very happy guide teaches us all to say,

'How *you* doin?' with an authentic Brooklyn accent. And we nail it, the whole bus does. True story.

Movie locations are pointed out as we go along the streets of Brooklyn, while the clips of the movies play on the screen in front of us. As we see John Travolta walking down a busy Brooklyn street in the opening scene of *Saturday Night Fever*, so do we, but on the TV on the bus. It is very cool. We are your normal tourists and don't mind the funny tourist routine from the tour guide. They do their spiels well!

First stop is Grimaldi's Coal Brick-Oven Pizzeria, which has the oldest pizza oven in Brooklyn and a feud that goes back generations with another pizza-making family. The line out the front is quite long, but as part of the pizza tour, we wander straight in. It is crowded, but the food comes out quickly. The thin crust pizza is hot and tasty, and afterwards we wander out to take photos of the city skyline.

The tour continues with L&B Spumoni Gardens pizzeria-restaurant, which is equally as packed as Grimaldi's. For those on the tour, we have an allocated spot, and soon the twenty-two of us are being served deep-dish pizza pie with tasty toppings and gelati. My preference is the thin base, so Grimaldi's is the winner!

Afterwards we finally see Coney Island, and although it's closed, we can now say we've been there. At least we know where it is now.

After saying goodbye to Kayla and Kelsey, who are heading home to Minnesota, a large group of us head downtown to see *Jersey Boys*, which is now not only one of my favourite musicals, but one of my favourite things I saw on the whole holiday. It is brilliant.

Our final days in New York City are filled with ice-skating and market shopping in Bryant Park, where Karen buys me a dachshund clock that looks just like Charlie, and I have my third dachshund sighting! It is a post-Christmas miracle. It is a tiny, chocolate brown puppy!

Dachshund Spotting Total:
Anthony 34, Maree 5, Holly 5.5, Sam 4.5, David 4, Lisa 3, Mum 1

There are carriage rides in Central Park, we play Ping Pong at SPiN, and we all abandon the children for an adults-only dinner, only our second in three months. We also visit FAO Schwartz toy store to step on the big piano keys like in the Tom Hanks' movie *Big*. As we leave to walk back to the subway, Sam spots a black, smooth haired miniature dachshund in Central Park. New York City has definitely delivered on the dachshunds.

Dachshund Spotting Total:
Anthony 34, Maree 5, Holly 5.5, Sam 5.5, David 4, Lisa 3, Mum 1

Welcoming in the New Year

We have one more day before we leave New York City for our week in Disney World. To say that the children (and a few of the adults) are excited is an understatement, but first we will see in the New Year altogether in New York City. It is a bitterly cold day, and I'm cold even in my new coat. Weather.com assures snow is coming but not yet. And even though we've had a few snowy experiences, I am so excited to see one last eddy of snow drifting around us in the late afternoon.

We all gather at my favourite pub, the New York City Beer Company, for a fabulous night with our family and friends. We don't quite make it to midnight at the pub with the younger children, but back at the hotel we ring in the New Year together.

I crawl in to bed just after midnight but can't sleep. I'm exhausted but happy, and so pleased with how well everything has gone in New York City. It's been full-on, exciting, and fun. It is exactly what I hoped for.

(23)

HOMEWARD BOUND

Date: *January 1*
Dachshunds so far: *58*

The Magic of Mickey

In what is a feat of absolute dumb luck, we manage to depart New York City twenty-four hours before a huge snowstorm hits the East Coast. A state of emergency is declared in New York as schools and airports are closed and hundreds of flights cancelled. For all my wishing for snow, I never wished for that much! It would have absolutely ruined some of our Disney World plans had we been stranded in New York City.

We hop on the Magic Bus at the Orlando airport, and one by one, each family checks in to the still festive Port Orleans Riverside Resort. What follows are days and days of fun-filled Disney joy. In groups of families we delight in the wonder of the Magic Kingdom, watch parades, buy Mickey Mouse ears, and smile through ride after ride. We spend a day at Hollywood Studios, watch shows, and eat at the 50's Prime Time Café. We all tour the Animal Kingdom, go on a safari through the savanna, and enjoy a day at Epcot. A special visit is made to Universal Studios for crazy coasters and the wonder of the Wizarding World of Harry Potter. We also spend a day at NASA for space exploration discovery and look for alligators in the Everglades. For young and old, Walt Disney World is a place of magic and a special treat for us all.

We didn't expect any dachshund spottings at Disney World since animals are not allowed in the parks, but we all know dachshunds are special, so when Mum tells me that she saw one outside the entry gates of Epcot, it doesn't surprise me at all. It's like they are following us around.

Dachshund Spotting Total:
Anthony 34, Maree 5, Holly 5.5, Sam 5.5, David 4, Lisa 3, Mum 2

As the days pass, I am no longer thinking of how many days of holiday we have left, but how many days until we arrive home.

Teary-Eyed and Time to Go Home

At the airport I lose it for the first time in three months. It starts at the check-in counter when we are not issued our boarding passes. We are told to pick them up at the gate. I've flown over a hundred times and Anthony more than three hundred, and we've never had to pick up our boarding passes at the gate. You check in, and you're supposed to be handed a boarding pass—that's how it works—but any queries about why we cannot have our passes are repeatedly ignored. We make our way to the gate to find that it is unattended until about fifteen minutes before boarding.

They advise over the loud speaker that the flight is overbooked and ask if anyone is willing to go on another flight. We begin to wonder whether this is why they're holding our boarding passes to ransom. Our bags are checked through to Sydney, and we are due at San Francisco airport for our next flight. We ask at the counter, but they still won't issue our passes, even though people are beginning to board. It is the first time on the holiday that I want to burst into tears.

When they finally issue them, as it is a 'through flight' to Sydney, we are handed two passes for all of us (Miami to San Fran and San Fran to Sydney), except Mum. When I ask where Mum's boarding pass is, they have no explanation whatsoever, except to say repeatedly, 'It hasn't issued, ma'am,' in a robotic voice.

The flight to San Francisco is the worst flight I've ever been on. We are placed in the very back row, which isn't an issue, but they run out of food, so we are starving when we arrive to San Francisco, only to find that nothing is open anywhere. I'm so worried that there won't be a seat for Mum on the next flight, so as we walk through the airport, I am almost in tears again. Anthony is by my side, always calm and always settling me if I get upset. 'It'll be all right,' he assures me as we make our way from the domestic terminal to the international.

It is very quiet in the terminal, like a ghost town, with rows and rows of empty seating and not many people about. We approach the United Airlines counter to enquire about Mum's seat. After all the kerfuffle at the Miami airport, her boarding pass is issued without a problem. I am so relieved, as is Mum.

Then Maree calls out suddenly, 'Dachshund!'

Are you kidding me? How is that possible?

We all stop. To our left are rows of empty seats, except one. Across the terminal a woman is sitting with a dachshund on her lap.

Tears fill my eyes as I look at the dachshund, the sixtieth of the trip. It is hard to believe that a dachshund has appeared at the last possible moment of the holiday, but there it is.

Final Dachshund Spotting Total:
Anthony 34, Maree 6, Holly 5.5, Sam 5.5, David 4, Lisa 3, Mum 2

'Not long now, Mum,' Holly tells me, her own eyes wet with tears.

'Only about eighteen hours.'

'Dad won the competition,' Sam remarks.

Maree smiles, commenting, 'I don't think there was ever any doubt.'

'He *is* the King of Dachshund Spotting,' I acknowledge.

Anthony grins and pops his arm around my shoulders. 'Told you.'

After eighty-eight days, fifteen countries, 54 thousand kilometres, and sixty dachshunds, it's time to go home.

Charlie

The flight and the car ride home feel longer than they should, but finally we pull into our driveway. As soon as the van door slides open, the four of us are out and racing over to Angela's next door, where Charlie has been staying for the last few days.

We knock on her back door and sing out, 'Hello.' Angela jumps up to greet us, and there is Charlie, as gorgeous as ever, playing with a dog toy. He doesn't notice us at first, but when he does, he drops the toy immediately and races over. He is beyond excited, as are we, and he doesn't know whom to go to first. He jumps at all of us, licking and whining over and over again. Like a typical dog, when Angela's dog tries to take the toy back, he is gone in a flash to guard what must be his current favourite toy. We call him to come home, but he won't leave without the toy. So over it comes to our house for the day.

It is so strange not to see Coco though. As we walk back across to our house, I can't help but glance to the bushes where we found her, but I don't stop. I don't want to think about that day, but I can't stop the tears. I feel like my heart is breaking. I pick Charlie up and cuddle him as we go inside.

'I want Coco,' Holly whispers as we walk inside the house.

'So do I, baby, so do I.' I glance at Coco's ashes sitting on the TV cabinet alongside a long-stemmed pink rose given to us by the vet. There is no high-pitched yowl as we walk through the house, and she is not here to launch into my arms and crawl up around the back of my neck. I swallow away the lump in my throat. It is simply awful to comprehend that she is not here. It is too quiet without her.

Charlie wags his tail and follows us around for more cuddles, but before long he climbs into his bed with the brown stuffed dog and snuggles up to it.

I take a deep breath and look around our house. Anthony draws me in for a cuddle. 'It's good to be home,' he says.

And it is. I loved every minute of our trip, except perhaps the boarding pass issue, but it is so good to be home.

Saying Good-Bye

It's weird to say goodbye to Maree and David as Anthony prepares to drop them home. We hug and talk of our amazing trip and how quickly it seems to have gone now that we are home. After being constant companions for three months, as the car pulls out of the driveway, I miss Maree and David already. Mum is still here, staying for a few days until she returns to her home, and I'm glad of that. I'm not ready for her to go yet. After months of company, I know it will be hard for her to go home to her quiet house, but like us, she is missing her home.

Home is constant; it is a comfort to our souls, but it is also where we face the reality of the ones that are not here with us. When moving through grief, we remember those who have passed, and those who have blessed our memories forever with love and laughter. Moving on is, and always will be, something that takes time, tears, and contemplation. I have lost my father, as has my sister, and Mum has lost the love of her life, but we have not lost his love. And Mum has come to terms with it in her own quiet way, but the holiday stirred it up again in ways she didn't realise. Through journaling, the love of family and friends, and an understanding, although unaccepting at times, that there are things we cannot change, her grieving is a gradual process, but she always looks to the future.

Death is absolute and unforgiving in its finality, but life? Life is a fragile thing, and we should give it our full attention, every day. I will keep my memories of Dad and Coco close to my heart, and other loved ones that have passed, but at the same time I choose to experience the joy of *right now*.

All of Those Things and More

My aim for the trip was met; quality time with Anthony and the kids, the parents and grandparents, and in the USA, time with more of the extended family. We saw the world, experienced new cultures, different climates, and learned the history of countries I didn't know much about. And Christmas markets, let's not forget the Christmas markets!

And it was all of those things, and more. My family and I have this wonderful shared experience that draws us closer together, and the friendship between Mum and Maree and David is truly a wonderful thing. They are now more than just relatives by marriage who got along well a few times a year at family gatherings; they are great friends who are now planning outings and holidays that don't involve Anthony and me. They don't need us! Ha!

There were times when it was harder travelling in a group than if it had been just Anthony and I and our children, but together, we managed it as we went along. Anthony learned that not everyone in a group likes walking at the speed of light, but neither do we have to amble leisurely—there is a happy medium that just needs to be discussed as a group, so everyone is happy. The biggest issue was that Anthony and I realised we needed more one-on-one time with Sam and Holly, so we did that. And in doing so, I think it forged the beginnings of the stronger friendship between Maree, David, and Mum. Not spending every minute together is key in successful group travel.

Anthony and I discovered that as the children grow older *our* outings and holidays need to be planned in collaboration with them. A holiday needs to satisfy all those travelling, and as much as Anthony, the grandparents, and I enjoyed the walking tours, it is definitely not a favourite activity for a twelve- and fifteen-year-old. Next time I may try and research an alternative way to learn about different cities and countries we visit. Not sure what that might be!

But I know this—I will never convince them to go on a walking tour ever again unless it involves chocolate or animals.

For me, I loved every minute spent travelling with my family. I laughed, cried, and experienced so much joy. I have a much broader knowledge about the world and its cultures, and I certainly have a deep sense of thankfulness about the life I have been given. It is a life full of love and opportunity and a bright future ahead. I have a home and food on the table, wonderful family and friends, and pets that warm my heart every day. It is a life free of war and terror. Not everyone is so lucky, and I do not want to take that for granted.

Pitter-Patter of Paws

A couple of days pass while we unpack and unwind. Charlie is quiet on his own, and unless we walk or play with him, he just lies quietly in his bed with the stuffed brown dog. And when outside, he whines at the fence to play with Angela's dog, Jessie. I sit down to search for a puppy, a girl, we have decided. After the busy days in New York City and Disney World, it has been weeks since I last looked for a puppy. After hours of searching every day, I find that nothing has changed. There are still none available.

In the midst of all the puppy searching, we read a feature article in the newspaper about the popularity of dachshunds in Australia now. It appears that between buying Coco and Charlie two years ago, dachshunds have become the new 'it' dog. The article advises that breeders have waiting lists months long.

I start to look farther afield and send emails to breeders all over Australia. Some put me on their waiting lists, others say their waiting lists are too long and aren't putting any more people on them, others are fussy, and I'm questioned before I can even go on a list.

I don't know what the rush is. We've only been home four days. I don't know why I need this so much. Is it for Charlie or me? But I can't let it go. I go back to searching.

Sam finds me in tears, really crying, in the kitchen one morning. After yet another phone call back from a breeder, although the website says they have a pup for sale, the breeder tells me they don't have *any* pups and the next two litters are allocated already.

'I can't find a puppy,' I bawl into Sam's chest.

Sam gives me a big cuddle. 'That's just not *our* puppy, Mum. We haven't found our puppy yet.'

This makes me sit up. He's right. I just haven't found *our* puppy yet.

Two more days pass during which I obsessively search. I call places that say they don't have any puppies, just in case. I leave messages with so many breeders that I carry my phone with me everywhere I go, even to the shower in case they call back. While I have shampoo streaming down my face, my phone rings.

I turn the shower off, grab my towel and the phone, and answer. It's a breeder from Queensland. She has a puppy, a female, tan smooth haired miniature that she was planning to show but has changed her mind. She has a waiting list, but my call came through at the moment she changed her mind. Her call was just for a chat at first. She is quite a discerning breeder and fussy about where her pups go, but once she hears our history with dachshunds, she offers me the pup. Minutes later an email comes through with a picture of her. She reminds me so much of Coco I burst into tears. I race through the house to tell the kids, 'We have a puppy!'

Unexpected Joys

Two days later I receive an email back from a breeder in South Australia—she sends a picture of a male, red smooth haired miniature dachshund, explaining that someone pulled out of a sale. Do we want him? One look at that pup, and I am in love.

I race outside with the iPad to Anthony who is gardening.

'How about *two* puppies?' I ask and show him the picture. He smiles. I think he realises it doesn't matter what his answer is.

After days of very lengthy discussions on names, we finally settle on 'Rosie' and 'Barney.' They are flying in from interstate, and we wait quite impatiently with the few other people expecting new puppies at Sydney airport. Before we know it, they arrive in dog crates, their little puppy faces peering from within. My heart melts. We gather them up and take turns for cuddles. I am in puppy heaven. In spite of all the knockbacks from breeders, within three weeks of arriving home from the holiday, we have two new babies.

Charlie doesn't know what's hit him. He does look slightly alarmed when we return home, giving us what looks like a 'What have you done to me?' look. After a few issues where Charlie thinks eating Barney for breakfast might be a good plan, and a muzzle is required, before too long there is play. Rosie is shy and a little quieter, but races around with the boys and growls for her favourite toy. And out of all the dachshunds we have ever cared for, we soon realise that Barney, like his namesake, Barney Stinson, may well be the cheekiest one of them all. Charlie is gentle with them, playing chase and settling them here and there with a firm paw. He looks happy again. After losing Coco and seeing Charlie so forlorn, we all find joy in this.

I am reminded again of Dad and how his death incited unexpected joy. His passing triggered our inviting Mum on our three-month holiday, then Maree and David, and in turn, the rest of our families for what really was a trip of a lifetime. And Coco's death led us here to these beautiful puppies. I wish she hadn't died on her own without us there to help her. It will play on my mind for a long time yet, I know, but I can't help but feel happiness at the sight of Rosie and Barney bonding with Charlie.

I sneak in and watch the three dogs in their bed on that first night, and I feel more at peace about Coco. The two puppies snuggle into Charlie, and I reach over to give him a pat. He licks my hand before laying his head across the puppies' tiny bodies, closing his eyes, and going to sleep.

I've arrived. Destination dachshund.

ACKNOWLEDGEMENTS

Thank you from the bottom of my heart to my family and friends who helped and supported me in the writing and publishing of *Destination Dachshund*. You *all* encouraged me, believed in me, and never let me give up.

A special thanks to my mother and daughter who helped me every step of the way - I couldn't have done it without you both.

Thank you to my family for such a wonderful holiday. It is something I will cherish forever. In expanding my travel blog to this memoir, I have relived every moment of our journey, reflected upon it, and experienced the heartache and the joy all over again. It truly was a 'once-in-a-lifetime' trip.

ABOUT THE AUTHOR

Lisa Fleetwood is a writer, blogger, book reviewer, and keen traveller. She lives in Sydney with her husband, two teen-age children, and three cheeky dachshunds. *Destination Dachshund* is her first book.

Visit Lisa's website and blog *Welcome to My Library* at www.lisafleetwood.com.au and join her in the discussion of books, travel, and dogs.

Follow Lisa on Twitter @LisaFleetwood or on Facebook at https://www.facebook.com/welcometomylibrary/

Download your free companion read for Destination Dachshund. Almost 100 pages of photos, maps, travel hints, and highlights: http://eepurl.com/cgVWfP

Bookends Publishing is a new Australian consultancy publisher. It came into being to help authors achieve their publishing dreams, provide publication advice to indie authors and opportunities for new, emerging, and established writers.

In 2017, the Bookends Australian Writing Award will be established to showcase Australian writers and their many talents. All shortlisted and winning entries will be published in an anthology.

http://bookendspublishing.com.au

Made in the USA
Middletown, DE
17 July 2019